JUST MY
TWO CENTS

JUST MY TWO CENTS

CHANSOO KIM, M.D.

authorHOUSE®

AuthorHouse™
1663 Liberty Drive
Bloomington, IN 47403
www.authorhouse.com
Phone: 1-800-839-8640

Published by AuthorHouse   06/30/2012

ISBN: 978-1-4685-6877-6 (sc)
ISBN: 978-1-4685-6876-9 (e)

Library of Congress Control Number: 2012905357

In Loving Memory of My Parents, the late
Mr. and Mrs. Do Won Kim

CONTENTS

INTRODUCTION

Two scores and seven years ago, I set foot on American soil in order to pursue my Postgraduate medical training at New York University Medical Center—Bellevue Hospital, New York City, New York. Now, looking back upon the vast time-span of the five decades gone by, I can hardly believe that our national landscape has undergone a sea change. According to an old Oriental adage, "Even Mother Nature changes in a decade's time," thus the inevitable changes have turned at least five times over beyond recognition. America as we know it today is a drastically different country from what we observed back in the 60's: many a thing that was acceptable back then is no longer even permissible, or downright illegal. Indeed, it goes without saying that the last half a century has been both tumultuous and cataclysmal in U.S. history.

I have lived in Springfield, IL for 38 years since 1974 in a professional move from Honolulu, Hawaii and I became a U.S. citizen in 1976 when we celebrated the Bicentennial. I am still very grateful to my adopted country for what she has done for me and my family. My two children were born, raised and educated in this blessed nation. Nothing gives me more pleasure and happiness than to see them vigorously strive for their own professional careers.

As we live in a diverse, pluralistic society, aptly called "melting pot" or "tossed salad," I, myself, am always determined to be an active Player in the Great American Game of Life rather than being an idle or passive spectator. For nearly quarter a century, whatever social issues or subjects might come along to grab my attention, I haven't hesitated to express my personal or professional opinion or viewpoint by writing to the Editor of newspapers, local and national, magazines, periodicals as well as professional journals. My letters and communications number altogether a little over 120. Now, I call them collectively, "JUST MY TWO CENTS." Most of them were published in the respective media, and my reader's responses, whether favorable or critical, are also included. If indicated, some references are provided for further elucidation.

I am well aware that my voice is feeble or hardly audible like a "voice in the wilderness." Yet, I believe that I leave behind my footprints on the Prairie that I have traversed thus far.

This book would not have come into existence without the loving and faithful support of my beloved wife, Young, who is always the source of my strength. My special thanks go to Aimie Trussell and Ms. Sara Barger who shared unselfishly their precious time with me in the preparation of the manuscript. I will always be grateful to them for their generous help.

February 20, 2012
Chansoo Kim, M.D.

S. KOREA MELEE
WAS A DISGRACE

(The State Journal-Register, October 2, 1988)

The eyes of the whole world are now fixed upon Seoul, Korea, the site of the 24th Olympiad. Needless to say, Korea's hosting of the games comes as icing on the cake as she is inching toward democratization. Its opening ceremony was spectacular beyond description.

Korea has once again demonstrated her ingenuity and prowess, flaunting to the entire world its miraculous economic comeback. Such a fantastic gala with opening ceremony has made us Korean-Americans proud of our Korean heritage.

Hardly a week into the Games enters a disgrace. I am now referring to a boxing match on September 22 and its ring melee that followed. A Korean boxer by the name of Byun Jong-Il plopped down in the ring for 67 minutes to protest against a 4-1 decision, thus earning the dubious reputation of a world record. The boxer felt the decision was grossly unfair and five other Korean officials even took part in the physical attack on referee Keith Walker.

I just happened to watch the match on TV. It's beyond the stretch of my wildest imagination that such a chaotic mob scene would ever take place at the gymnasium. I don't believe any decent person could shrug it off as one of those lapses of knee-jerk reaction and confusion. As one of the anchormen quipped, "A gold medal for the worst behavior goes to the hosting country." I would say that this most unfortunate incident has brought out the worst in Koreans. It amounts to their national disgrace.

We were and still are worried about ever-present dangers of sabotage against the Olympics from Communist North Korea. Ironically, South Koreans have so far found their worst enemy inside and among themselves. This boxing mishap already cost the president of the Korean Olympic Committee (KOC) his job. They are reported to be looking into possible legal action against the coaches and boxer involved.

It is our fervent wish that the Korean image abroad won't be tarred with the same brush. We pray that Korea conclude the Olympic Games with a bang, not a whimper.

WE'RE ALL UPROOTED

(Illinois Times, December 1-7, 1988)

The featured article of the November 10-16, 1988 Illinois Times by Maija Devine (See "Seoul food") had the Korean community literally "up in arms." I also find the article smacking of much self-serving, being loaded with misinformation, prejudices, and flagrant arrogance to the point of bigotry. The story reminds one of the proverbial blindmen and the elephant.

I am further dismayed to learn that the author's views represent the antithesis of Christianity. Her quotation from *The Uprooted* by Oscar Handlin is undoubtedly misplaced here and utterly out of context. After all, we are all "uprooted", not in the physical sense but spiritually. "Korean immigrants, Christian and non-Christian alike gather on Sundays at the Korean Presbyterian Church to seek refuge from the anguish of the world."

The very word of sanctuary of a church means nothing but a place of refuge or protection. As Christians, we are not ashamed at all, rather we are very proud, to declare that we turn to God, of all things, to seek His refuge from the anguish of the world. We are not alone and for that matter, not singular. By so doing, we join the World Community of Christianity. Our invigorating spiritual strength can help us keep clear of social ills, notably alcohol and drug abuse which has now become a national crisis of the first magnitude.

The author continues to argue that Korean immigrant's inherent sense of "alienation and their high frustration level" have caused "near obsession with their children's education." However, it is a matter of common knowledge that Korea, our Motherland, enjoys

3

an extremely high literacy rate of well over 90 percent, non-pareil to any other Western nation. Can anyone, including the author, even attribute this highly desirable record to their sense of alienation and frustration? We have been imbued with the value of education, and ignorance is often decried as our worst enemy. Yes, we stress education just as much as work ethic.

As with any other ethnic groups or communities, some of the Koreans are in the professions, others run their own businesses, to name a few, restaurants, beauty parlors, auto repair shops, etc. But we never regard one profession over the other, nor do we value one occupation above the other. We believe jobs are only as good as job holders are. At least in our view, no job is considered menial or low.

We Korean-Americans aspire to be the spitting image of WASPs. We all are a hard-working, proud and devout people, and every one of them believes in the American success story.

INAUGURATION
IS A TESTIMONIAL

(The State Journal-Register, January 31, 1989)

Inaugural ceremony is often regarded as a "rite of passage" in the government or simply a change of guard every four years. Some people even berate the inauguration's extravagance, which seems to be somewhat understandable in view of our burgeoning budget deficit and the homeless roaming the streets.

Yet, we should in no way overlook or belittle its historic significance; no other nation on Earth has ever achieved and continued such a peaceful and orderly succession of government for 200 years and that without interruption.

This is a monumental testimony to America's steadfast commitment and dedication to lofty ideals and principles of democracy.

I have watched six inaugural ceremonies altogether from Lyndon B. Johnson on down. Each time it generates unabated awesome feelings about people's ultimate power, reaffirming my faith in our political system and offering a unique challenge to me as a naturalized citizen.

Across the Pacific, in the Far East, abominable political scenarios are now unfolding; deposed dictators either have gone into exile or are scurrying into a hiding place. Ours is the only nation which to this day stands tall and proud as the last hope and bulwark of freedom.

Reader's Response

IMPERIAL DISPLAY DEPRIVES NEEDY

(The State Journal-Register, February 10, 1989)

Dear Editor:

I would like to express my disagreement with Dr. Chansoo Kim and his viewpoint on the inaugural ceremony. It is hard to understand how anyone can call spending $25 million on the inauguration a commitment to democracy. Dr. Kim added insult to injury by first referring to the budget deficit and the homeless.

Someone should do a survey to find out how much warmer the homeless felt sleeping under newspapers reporting this great use of the people's money. Imagine the joy of America's working poor and the delight of the average taxpayer at this succession to more useless spending.

I agree with Dr. Kim's faith in our system, and share his pride in America's stand for hope and freedom. But I believe that, instead of patting our leaders on the back for staging an imperial show to change leaders, we prod them elsewhere. With enough prodding maybe everyone will get a larger piece of the American pie.

Sam Short
Edinburg

DILANTIN TOXICITY AND DEPRESSION

Arch Phys Med Rehabil Vol 71, November 1990

Letters to the Editor

Dilantin toxicity and depression

I read with misgivings the report by Drs. Garrison and Henson[1] of two cases associated with Dilantin toxicity and depression. The authors either have failed or have neglected to recognize the critical role of drug interaction. Both of their patients were on multiple medications, including cimetidine and over-the-counter decongestants. To my dismay, the authors state "To our knowledge, neither of these have been reported to have an effect on Dilantin levels." Yet those two cases, in my opinion, illustrate unequivocally, drug interaction of Dilantin and cimetidine.

Cimetidine is associated with several notorious drug interactions because of its effect on inhibiting the cytochrome P450 hepatic enzyme system. This enzyme system is responsible for metabolizing a variety of drugs, including anti-convulsants (Phenytoin & Carbamazepine), Theophylline, Warfarin (Coumadin), etc. Concomitant administration of cimetidine with these drugs can limit their metabolism and result in accumulation with the potential induction of drug toxicity. Cimetidine inhibition of drug metabolism is believed to be of immediate onset and offset once therapy is discontinued, and is dose related.

Therefore, to avoid adverse side-effects, close monitoring with adjustment of Dilantin dosage is strongly recommended.

Chansoo Kim, MD

Springfield, IL 62703

Reference

1. Garrison SJ, Henson HK: Dilantin toxicity and vegetative depression: a report of two cases. Arch Phys Med Rehabil 1990; 71:422–423.

DILANTIN TOXICITY AND DEPRESSION

Arch Phys Med Rehabil Vol 71, November 1990

The authors reply

Medication interactions should always be suspected in cases of drug toxicity. Though cimetidine, through inhibition of hepatic metabolism, does increase serum phenytoin concentration, a steady state serum phenytoin level is achieved in days to several weeks. The interest in these two cases should not stem simply from the mechanism of development of toxicity, but rather the discovery of vegetative depression as the presenting sign of Dilantin toxicity. Both of the reported cases experienced no medication changes while on cimetidine and Dilantin. More importantly, they had been in therapeutic ranges each time tested prior to discharge from the hospital. Regardless of concurrent medications, Dilantin levels should be evaluated prior to the initiation of antidepressant therapy in patients who become clinically depressed.

Susan J. Garrison, MD

Helene K. Henson, MD
Baylor College of Medicine
Houston, TX 77030

OPINION ON
ACCENTED ENGLISH

(Illinois Times, March 9-15, 1991)

I read Kim Buford's article ("See Minorities Challenge DOT Class . . . . ," IT, April 25, 1991) with much foreboding concern.

The thrust of debate centers around a proposed class which allegedly aims at curbing accents of some foreign-born employees at one of the state agencies.

First and foremost, if it is, indeed, true that some of targeted state employees have worked for the past fifteen to twenty years without demonstrable communication problems, what on earth could possibly have triggered this urgent need to improve or shed their foreign accents now? It sounds as if their English had steadily deteriorated over time due to some mysterious illness.

Granted, there is always room, although more often among aliens than natives, for improvement on communication skills, let alone accents or voice articulation problems.

Yet, one shouldn't forget or overlook the fact that all foreign-born state employees are bilingual, thus being on the cutting edge of not only our ethnically diverse society but also our emerging global economy.

I find myself in total disagreement with Sandra Kaikumba's remark that "a slight accent can become a barrier."

On the national scene, two most eminent American politicians known worldwide for their renowned scholarship, immediately come to mind; they are none other than Dr. Henry Kissinger and Zbigniew Brzezinski. We notice that they speak with a mild accent, if not thick or heavy. Yet, both of them have served the nation with honor and distinction in the capacity of national security advisor to the president, and Dr. Kissinger as the most distinguished secretary of state. Locally, we have Mayor Ossie Langfelder who has just won reelection on his own merits. His accented English seems to make him all the more attractive. This brouhaha over the issue of accented English makes me naturally wonder loud and clear about the future of our second generation Asian-Americans, who were born, raised, and educated here and who speak immaculate English.

STUDENTS PRAISED FOR USING RACE RIOT AS TOPIC

(The State Journal-Register, June 17, 1991)

It is by far heartening to read that two sixth-graders at Iles School chose, of all subjects, Springfield race riots of 1908 as part of their history project in a statewide competition under the joint sponsorship for the Illinois Historic Preservation Agency and the Illinois State Historical Society.

Not only are these lovely youngsters to be commended for the "excellent" rating on their fine project, but their historic perspective is amazingly revealing and inspirational to all of us.

This remarkable piece of their work, coupled with their singlehanded petition drive to the city council, help raise our hopes high for the bright future of our younger generation despite all the horror stories to the contrary.

It is often said that history repeats itself, but our two young children challenge us not to let the 1908 tragedy be repeated. It's just admirable that young as they are they strive to stand for fairness, justice and equality in our society. After all, that's exactly what America is all about.

Not long ago, Japan as a nation made an embarrassing attempt to tinker with her infamous past history of naked aggression, triggering a wave of angry protests from the four corners of the earth.

My hat is off to Lindsay Harney and Amanda Staab for the job well done, from whom we have much to learn.

THE STATE
Journal Register
A SPRINGFIELD CENTURY

◆ AUGUST 14, 1908 ◆

'Riot sparked by event that never happened

No crime ever committed in Springfield had such widespread repercussions as the report of a sexual assault on Mabel Hallam on the night of Aug. 13, 1908.

Her accusation was the spark that ignited the Springfield Race Riot and led to the deaths of seven people, injuries to scores of others and the destruction of an entire neighborhood of black homes and businesses.

It also was a crime that never actually happened.

Hallam claimed that she had been asleep in her bed about 11:30 p.m. the evening of the attack.

Her husband, Earl, a streetcar driver, was still at work.

Mabel Hallam said a black man entered her home while she was asleep, came into her bedroom, choked her and dragged her into the back yard, where he assaulted her. Her screams brought neighbors, who helped her and called the police.

The police rounded up all the "suspicious negroes" they could find, including one George Richardson, a 36-year-old la-

borer with a criminal record who had been working in the vicinity of the Hallam home.

Although Hallam was unable to identify Richardson as her assailant on two occasions, she later told authorities she was "positive he is the one" who attacked her.

Many local whites were outraged by the attack on Hallam, and their anger was fanned by coverage of the event in the Illinois State Register. The paper placed heavy emphasis on the racial aspect of the crime and did its best to demonize the perpetrator even before he was identified.

The Register never referred to the supposed attacker as an "assailant" or even just a "man."

Instead, the word "negro" was constantly repeated, except when even more emotionally charged terms, such as "fiend" or "villain," were employed.

The Register called the attack "one of the greatest outrages that ever happened in Springfield" and an assault of "exceptional brutality and brazenness."

A later historian would term the Register's coverage "clearly inflammatory."

Spurred in part by such reporting, a mob formed, determined to lynch Richardson and another black who was housed in the county jail on charges he had murdered a white man. When the two were spirited away to safety, the mob turned its attentions to the black community at large, rioting, burning and looting for two nights in a row and devastating a large section of town.

Two weeks after the alleged assault on Mabel Hallam, she told authorities that Richardson was not the man who attacked her and gave them the description of another black man.

Later, she told a special grand jury that she had not been attacked by a black man at all, but had instead been with her white lover.

Richardson was released from jail and returned to his life in Springfield, but the city would never be quite the same again.

Partly as a result of the riot, the National Association for the Advancement of Colored People was formed in 1909.

The Hallam family reportedly left Springfield a few months after the riot.

Dragged From Her Bed And Outraged By Negro

MRS. EARL HALLAM OF 1153 N. FIFTH ST.
VICTIM OF BRUTAL ASSAULT

CARRIED FROM HOME BY NEGRO

CHOKED INTO INSENSIBILITY BY VILLIAN WHO GAINED ENTRANCE THROUGH THE KITCHEN — DEED COMMITTED IN BACK YARD

NO CLEW REACHED AS TO PERPETRATOR

One of the greatest outrages that ever happened in Springfield took place about 11:30 o'clock last night, when Mrs. Earl Hallam, 1153 North Fifth street, was dragged from her bed into the yard at the rear of her home and criminally assaulted by an unidentified negro.

THE ILLINOIS STATE REGISTER
AUG. 14, 1908

THE SPRINGFIELD RACE RIOT OF 1908

CONCLUSION: GENESIS OF NAACP

By Sunday morning, much of Springfield laid in ruins. On Sunday more national guard troops arrived and in general the day was peaceful. The official death total was reported to be seven, two blacks and five accidental whites. It was rumored that there were many more deaths and others as a result of the riot. Property damage was in excess of $200,000. Forty homes were destroyed and others were damaged while twenty-four businesses were forced to close their doors either temporarily or permanently.

Immediately after the riot, city officials expressed deep regret for the mob's actions and called for swift justice. The call for justice was left unanswered as the 107 indictments returned by the special grand jury granted only one conviction and that was for someone who stole a saber from one of the guards. The murders of Scott Burton and William Donnegan were left unpunished as were the arsonists who set fire to the homes in the Badlands. Kate Howard, one of the ringleaders of the mob, decided to commit suicide rather than face charges. Mabel Hallam later told the authorities she made up the story about being raped in order to cover up an affair she was having. George Richardson was therefore released from jail, but Joe James was tried and convicted of the murder of Clergy Ballard.

The Springfield Race Riot of 1908 was sparked by Mabel Hallam's false accusation and fueled by economic and racial tension already brewing in the black and white communities. This riot also marked the last conflict between the races when the black people did not rise up as a group to defend themselves. As a possible result of the riots in the Great Emancipator's home town, an integrated group of concerned citizens gathered in the Big Apple, New York City. This group was seeking a solution to the growing problems between the blacks and the whites in America. How could a city that prided itself on the home of the man who set the slaves free also try to run blacks out of their town? **If this could happen in Springfield, Illinois, it could happen anywhere in the United States. Something had to be done. This idea gave rise to the National Association For The Advancement of Colored People (NAACP).** Today, as the most influential civil rights organization, it continues to strive for the civil liberties of African Americans.

KOREAN COMMUNITY

(Chicago Tribune, July 19, 1991)

I was shocked to read the front-page article "Local Korean politics is Chicago all the way," in the Tribune (June 30).

Recent scandal-ridden campaigns for president of Chicago's Korean-American Association and fraudulent election charges that followed have brought crying shame to all Koreans in Illinois and tarnished the image of the entire Korean community.

One of the candidates openly claimed that he is "not seeking an honor or award or recognition," but striving to provide "strictly service" to the community.

Under the circumstances, the best service that both candidates could possibly render is to gracefully have their names withdrawn, so that a new election may be held for new leadership of the Korean Society.

ZACHARY TAYLOR VERDICT
A SERVICE TO THE NATION

(The State Journal-Register, July 22, 1991)

American democracy has scored big with the long-awaited verdict that Zachary Taylor, the 12th U.S. President, was not poisoned by arsenic as widely speculated among some historians. The century-old wild rumors surrounding the "mysterious" death of Taylor have finally been laid to rest.

Now, it is medically proven beyond reasonable doubt that Taylor died of natural causes (gastroenteritis) on July 9, 1850. Thanks to the Kentucky coroner's office, "historical villains" behind the Taylor case, namely Henry Clay, Jefferson Davis and Millard Fillmore, have been vindicated.

In this connection, Kentucky's medical examiner has done a great service to the nation in general and the descendants in particular of those falsely accused political leaders of circa 1850. Dr. George Nichols, Kentucky's chief examiner, said it all, "We have truth and that's what we were after."

Needless to say, his terse remark reflects the quintessence of the noble American spirit which never ceases to seek truth out, no matter how long it may take. Our uncompromising faith that truth should see the light of day sets our country apart from the rest of the world.

NAUSEOUS VS. NAUSEATED

(Illinois Medicine, August 2, 1991)

At the risk of being branded a pendant, I ask that you note the inappropriate use of the word "nauseous" [in the "Case in Point," June 21 issue]. The patient, were he still alive, might very well sue for defamation of personality!

David B. Littman, M.D.
Highland Park

Editor's note: Dr. Littman, the newest member of the Illinois Medicine committee, was not alone in catching our error. Donald G. Parkhurst, M.D., of Kankakee, also noted the incorrect use of "nauseous," meaning "Causing nausea," instead of "nauseated," which means "suffering from nausea."

PENDANT VS. PEDANT

Letter to the Editor

August 5, 1991

Letters to the Editor
Illinois Medicine
Twenty North Michigan Avenue
Suite 700
Chicago, IL 60602

Dear Editor:

At the risk of being branded as a nitpicker, I bring to your attention with some misgivings to what obviously appears to be a humorous typo in Illinois Medicine (August 2nd issue). It's now "pendant vs. pedant" rather than "nauseous vs. nauseated."

Dr. David B. Littman seems to be in a no-win situation. But a light moment is always good medicine.

Chansoo Kim, M.D.
Springfield, IL

The American Heritage Guide to Contemporary Usage and Style—2005 by Houghton Mifflin

nauseous/nauseated/nauseating

Traditional usage lore has insisted that *nauseous* should be used only to mean "causing nausea" and that it is incorrect to use it to mean "feeling sick to one's stomach." Back in 1965, the Usage Panel was in step with this thinking, with 88 percent rejecting the "feeling sick" meaning of *nauseous*.

This attitude persisted for decades but has since begun to give way. In our 1988 survey, 72 percent of the Panel thought that a roller coaster should be said to make its riders *nauseated* rather than *nauseous*. A decade later, however, the Panel's attitude has changed dramatically. In our 1999 survey, 61 percent of the Panel approved of the sentence *Roller coasters make me nauseous.*

This change might have been inevitable once people began to think that *nauseous* did not properly mean "causing nausea" as traditional lore would have it. Even in our 1988 survey, this was the case, as 88 percent preferred nauseating in the sentence *The children looked a little green from too many candy apples and nauseating (not nauseous) rides.* The 1999 results for this same example were not significantly different.

Since there is abundant evidence for the "feeling sick" use of *nauseous*, the word presents a classic example of a word whose traditional, "correct" usage is being supplanted by a newer, "incorrect" one. In other words, what was now considered an error is becoming standard practice.

SCHOOL PHOBIA

(Excerpted from The Wall Street Journal's
front-page article, September 3, 1991)

.... "The unfamiliar terror often comes on suddenly. One school phobia from New York, who asked not to be named, still hasn't figured out what hit him seven years ago on the morning of the third day of sixth grade. Then a 10 year old who had scarcely missed a single day of school, he refused to get out of his mother's car. <u>Dizzy and nauseous at the mere thought of school</u>, he stayed home for most of the next month, seeing a battery of physicians and psychiatrists. Still, the condition lasted the rest of the year. Only home tutoring kept him up with his studies." ....

SCHOOL PHOBIA-NAUSEOUS VS NAUSEATED

September 4, 1991

Letters to Editor
Wall Street Journal
Dow Jones & Company, Inc.
200 Liberty Street
New York, NY 10281

At the risk of being branded as a pedant, may I direct your attention to the incorrect use of the word nauseous in "School Phobia" (Sept. 3, 1991). To be nauseous or nauseated, that is a question.

To set the record straight, "nauseous" means "causing nausea" and "nauseated" means suffering from nausea."

Chansoo Kim, M.D.
Springfield, IL

SCHOOL PHOBIA

(Editor's Response, October 14, 1991)

THE WALL STREET JOURNAL.   DOW JONES & COMPANY, INC.
Publishers
200 LIBERTY STREET — NEW YORK, N. Y. 10281

PAUL R. MARTIN
ASSISTANT TO THE MANAGING EDITOR

October 14, 1991

Chanson Kim, M.D.
619 South Fourth Street
Springfield, Illinois 63703

Dear Dr. Kim:

Thank you for your September 4th letter about the
misuse of "nauseous" in the Journal.

Webster's New World Third Edition, among other
dictionaries, now do allow the use meaning affected
by nausea--nauseated. We try to stick to the old
usage, but misuses do creep in.

We appreciate your interest. We know that readers
like you hold us to high standards, and we try to
live up to these expectations.

Sincerely,

Paul R. Martin

PM/kc

23

PARENTS MUST BE PART
OF EDUCATION REFORM

(The State Journal-Register, September 22, 1991)

Popular as it may be among politicians, a voucher system alone will not vouch for better education of our children. Nor would a school choice program be a panacea for all our problems with school reform.

Education is, and always should be a joint project between parents, teachers and students. Whatever is achieved in classrooms could easily be lost at home.

In order to gain some insights into the fundamental deficiency of our educational system, one needs to look no further than Southeast's recent incident. As reported in the local papers, a veteran English teacher is being penalized allegedly for a high "fail" rate in her class.

It is encouraging and at once very heartening though, to see some of her former students speak up for and stand by their ace teacher. I find it rather hard to understand why both parents and students have been so reticent about the school's insensibly harsh action taken against their most valuable teacher.

Parents must become well informed about their schools and actively involved in what they do. Schools are somewhat supposed to be what parents and students want them to be.

No education reform would be meaningful or successful without parents' active participation and cooperation and their vigilant efforts to improve their children's education.

THE "BURNING" LEAF ISSUE NEEDS TO BE RESOLVED

(The State Journal-Register, October 15, 1991)

Every year, as we enter fall season, we invariably confront the ever-present leaf burning issue as a "rite of passage."

Unfortunately, this volatile issue of yard and lawn waste disposal has been with us for as long as I remember, and we have gone through the proverbial maze of "creative" yard waste disposal methods from biodegradable to clear bags to stickers to paper waste disposal bags, etc.

As yet, no permanent solution has been offered to Springfield residents or is in sight.

Much to our dismay, it is now reported that the City Council voted unanimously to table the leaf-burning ordinance and that we will most likely be asked to vote on this "burning question" in the future.

As things stand now, the City Council leaves us practically hung up in air and we can't help but feel we are getting shortchanged.

I deeply deplore the council's foot-dragging and wishy-washy approach toward the essential service of leaf disposal. Enough is enough! Springfield residents certainly deserve better treatment from their elected aldermen.

DEMOCRATIC PROCESS HAYWIRE AT HEARINGS

(The State Journal-Register, November 17, 1991)

In medicine, postmortem examination is often acclaimed to be a teacher's teacher. Postmortem of the Thomas Hearings could be just as rewarding and may shed some light on how our democratic process on Capitol Hill went haywire.

The outcome of unprecedented public Senate inquisition is that Judge Thomas walks into the Supreme Court as Associate Justice with a cloud over his head, and that Professor Hill's credibility and even her sanity remain seriously challenged.

In the meantime, some of our senators are busy pointing the finger at each other for their disastrous handling of the confirmation hearings. As a result, there is no denying that democracy in America has had better days.

Judge Hoerchner as a witness concluded her shaky opening statement with a petition from her Yale classmates. Ironically, some distinguished senators of the Judiciary committee deliberately and repeatedly implied during the hearings that one's integrity has something to do with one's academic achievement or credentials. This perception is fatally flawed and the American public finds it hard to swallow.

To add insult to injury, Senator Metzenbaum even queried a panel of Thomas character witnesses, "What do you think of 66 Yale Law School graduates all over the country and even from overseas, and their joint petition submitted here in defense of Professor Hill's integrity and character?"

I dare to answer that the senator's question in itself is ridiculously irrelevant and that the sleazy unsworn petition is just as valid as a lie detector.

The very fact that an accuser is an elite with a Yale degree doesn't add an iota to his or her credibility. The burden of proof ultimately falls on the accuser, be he an Ivy League graduate or Joe Six-Pack with a G.E.D.

My question is, "Where does this leave Honest Abe?" We all know that Abraham Lincoln is no Yale Law School graduate. He has not even received a formal education as such. He taught himself to be a lawyer and yet he has become the greatest president in our history.

Ours is a "show me" country and we don't take anything for granted. We believe democratic process is not "lousy" but fair. Democracy is the best form of government, if properly run.

JAPANESE MUST ACT TO ACCEPT RESPONSIBILITY

(The State Journal-Register, December 23, 1991)

Of all monuments, the USS Arizona Memorial holds a very special place in our hearts. The observance of the 50th anniversary of the Japanese attack on Pearl Harbor brings us all a painful flashback.

Even half a century later, the memory of Pearl Harbor is fresh to its survivors. However, the solemnity of the occasion dictates that we refrain from Japan-bashing or badmouthing her with invectives.

This particular commemorative event appears to be at a watershed, given the following compelling facts.

1. Japan, as a redoubtable economic powerhouse, is pretty soon to be equipped with a strong offensive military machine, raising the specter of rising militarism;
2. With the tacit approval of the Japanese government, the Japanese have willfully revised their history books, despite an outburst of anger and protests from their neighboring countries. Thanks to their masterly "sanitization" process, Japan's past history of naked aggression may now look benign to their offsprings;
3. Demographically, the majority of people on both sides of the Pacific were born after the Pearl Harbor attack, and its hard-won lessons might not sink in with them.

It is quite incomprehensible that most of the Japanese tend to regard themselves as the victims of the World War II, especially due to U.S. atomic bombings of Hiroshima and Nagasaki. They seem understandably preoccupied with their own past sufferings, and yet they are still so reluctant to confront their ugly history to the extent where some of them demand unabashedly that apologies be reciprocated.

Why should we apologize to them for being savagely attacked in the early otherwise peaceful morning of December 7, 1941?

We live in what they call a global village. To be accepted as a trustworthy partner, it takes Japan more than a simple apology.

PEACE GESTURE BY NORTH KOREA IS A CRUEL HOAX

(The State Journal-Register, January 8, 1992)

Coupled with the triumphant victory of the gulf war and the dramatic demise of the once most powerful and oppressive "evil empire" of the Soviet Union, the news that North Korea has finally signed a pact of non-aggression and reconciliation with South Korea seems to augur well for the future, at least on the political front.

What is most perplexing is that Dictator Kim Il Sung, a Saddam Hussein in the Far East, who is hell-bent on developing nuclear weapons, suddenly changes his tune, extending an olive branch toward the government of South Korea, his sworn archenemy since 1950.

For one thing, North Korea is widely reported to be financially in dire straits, reeling under the weight of its mounting foreign debt. On the other hand, Pyongyang finds itself confronting single handedly the entire world that rises up against its nuclear program.

Thus, the communists in the North, in a desperate move to defuse the explosive level of tensions on the peninsula, resorted to having a series of dialogues with Seoul which culminated in a "toothless" non-aggression pact.

This peace gesture from North Korea will turn out to be not only a cruel hoax but a sheer political ploy whereby they are wishfully trying to have a breathing spell for their imminent economic collapse and at the same time to ward off unceasing calls for international inspection of their nuclear facility.

It is feared that South Korea would be in for a rude awakening once again, for the non-aggression treaty in itself is hardly worth more than the paper its printed on unless North Korea agrees unconditionally to nuclear inspections and safeguards.

Unfortunately, the prospect of reunification of both Koreas could be as remote as it has ever been.

WE MUST GET REALISTIC IN DEALING WITH JAPAN

(The State Journal-Register, January 24, 1992)

Hardly a day passes by without our hearing of thousands of Americans losing their jobs as unemployment continues to soar. Congress is now clamoring for stimulative federal programs such as public work projects to get the floundering economy back on its feet.

Indeed, the current economic picture is so bleak that people are scared to spend money. We need no one to tell us that we have fallen on hard times.

In the midst of our deepening recession, how ironic it is that Los Angeles County Transportation Commission, despite a lower bid by a U.S. firm, has awarded Sumitomo Corp., a Japanese concern, a juicy contract for their new mass transit Metro Line. We all know that no nation can match us for technological know-how.

Some years ago, Japan had a multi-billion dollar construction project going and some topflight American construction companies rushed to get in with their unsurpassed skills and expertise for a piece of the action. But they got practically shut out.

When President Bush traveled to Tokyo with his entourage of leading U.S. business executives, we were referred to as "a friend in need" by the Japanese prime minister. They acted as if we were there to have a few bones thrown at us. What we ask for are level-playing fields, not a "hand-out" or table "crumbs".

A free and fair trade policy means nothing to the Japanese but a restrictive and managed trade policy for them. When we say "live and let live", they respond with "live and let die". Are we as a nation losing our grip with reality? Where is our good old mother wit?

LET'S WORK TO KEEP OUR NATION ALIVE AND WELL

(The State Journal-Register, February 7, 1992)

Dear Editor,

Raise the red, white and blue for Dr. Chansoo Kim for his apt comments on being realistic in dealing with Japan. It seems as though too many people have the misconception that Japanese products are better than American ones.

Not only has Japan gotten its foothold in the automobile market, but also in real estate. Would it be possible that in the near future we will have to learn Japanese because they will be governing this country?

It seems as though the American people have forgotten the struggle and sacrifices our ancestors experienced in fighting obstacles to make this a free and self-sustaining country where everyone can freely voice their opinions, vote however they want and worship however they wish.

Let's get off of "let Japan have it" and keep America alive and well.

Norma M. Derteano
Springfield

PRAISES DISABILITIES ACT FOR ITS IMPACT

(The State Journal-Register, May 12, 1992)

Americans with Disabilities Act, signed by President Bush in July, 1990, is hailed as the most comprehensive legislation of its kind, and the historical significance is comparable with the Civil Rights Act of 1964.

Undoubtedly, ADA represents a quantum leap toward full participation in American society by 43 million people with disabilities. The act is indeed the culmination of relentless social changes over 30 years to accommodate disabilities that had been set in motion by our visionary leader, the late John F. Kennedy, when he promulgated that all new public buildings be architecturally wheelchair accessible and barrier-free.

The University of Illinois at Urbana-Champaign still enjoys the reputation for being the first institution of higher learning in the nation, where they have enrolled students with disabilities even in the early '60s. Illinoisans can justifiably take pride in the fact that their prestigious state institution has been in the forefront.

Non-employment accommodation requirements under the ADA took effect Jan. 26, 1992. Employment provisions are scheduled to take effect July 26, 1992. Full compliance as required by the ADA could very well turn out to be a difficult transition period, particularly in these tough economic times. But it certainly deserves our cooperation to the fullest extent with the implementation of the Act.

No other nation has come this far in creating a barrier-free society for persons with disabilities.

FOREIGN ACCENTS IN AMERICAN CORPORATE SUITES

(Wall Street Journal, May 29, 1992)

It is with some apprehension that I read the Wall Street Journal's article, "Foreign Accents Proliferate in Top Ranks of U.S. Companies" (5/21/92).

In this day and age of global economy, foreign accents heard increasingly at all-American corporate suites shouldn't come as a surprise, much less a threat to U.S. businesses.

The fact of the matter is our society overall tends to be far more tolerant of Europeans' accents than those of non-Caucasians, specifically Asians.

Years ago, a noted Japanese-American author, a Nisei, had the occasion to deliver a speech and there happened to be a U.S. Senator in the audience. Later, while approaching the Japanese writer with unstinting praise, the senator blurted out an inscrutable question, where did you learn such an impeccable English?"

Is this to be taken as a compliment or an insult?

A foreigner's accent is one thing. Stereotyping is another thing, which is a subtle form of racism.

The heightened awareness of foreign accents makes me wonder again, loud and clear, about the future of our second generation Asian-Americans who are born, raised and educated here and who speak flawless English.

OUR PATCHWORK

(Chicago Tribune, June 21, 1992)

The Tribune's articles on Asian-Americans and Keith J. Lencho's recent response prompt me to make the following comments.

It is somewhat appalling to see a gross error in the definition of the "1.5 generation." The 1.5 generation, as opposed to the second generation, refers to those Koreans who were not born in this country but have been raised and educated here.

American society used to be referred to as a melting pot. However, from the modern sociologic perspective, the term is rather antiquated and conceptually flawed. It should be replaced by "salad bowl" or "patchwork quilt," whereby diverse ethnic groups are expected not only to retain their identity but to preserve their tradition and cultural heritage, thus enriching our vibrant multiculture all the more.

Mr. Lencho complained that a Korean herb purveyor's sign is in Korean. As long as we run our business within legal boundaries, who on earth dares dictate the type and nature of our signs or which segment of the population we target as our customers?

This is regrettably another telltale sign among some Americans of deep-seated intolerance of ethnic diversity in our country.

JAPANESE SLOW TO ADMIT THEIR WRONGS

(The State Journal-Register, July 17, 1992)

Japanese people are swift as an arrow to put out all kinds of gizmos on the world market, but they are lamentably slow as molasses to admit their past wrongs.

The latest hot potato involves "comfort women" Imperial Japan duped and dragooned to service their troops in World War II. The victims of dastardly sex-slavery are reported to number anywhere from 100,000 to 200,000, and most of them were Korean women and teenaged girls.

After 47 years of stonewalling and six months investigation, Japan finally admitted July 6 that its government had been involved in setting up a vast network of military brothels during the war. Prime Minister Miyazawa formally apologized to the Korean people for their despicable wartime behavior.

As a first grade school boy, I still remember my sixth grade neighbor girl having been recruited as a "comfort woman" to Manchuria.

How ironic it is that Mr. Miyazawa, a graduate of the most elite Tokyo Imperial University, could take this long to come to grips with another sordid piece of their past history. Once again, Japan's much delayed confession brings their collective conscience into question.

A MOMENT OF PRIDE
FOR KOREAN-AMERICANS

(The State Journal-Register, August 16, 1992)

The 25th Olympic Games in Barcelona, Spain, ended Sunday with fanfare. They are now being hailed as the most memorable games ever played by mankind in recent memory. Each competing nation, new and old, large and small, has shown itself at its very best during the Games.

One of the most poignant and unforgettable sagas unfolded on the final day, when a young Korean athlete by the name of Hwang Young-Cho crossed the finish line to win the men's marathon. Although barely known to the public, this is the second time Korea has won the Olympic marathon. In 1936, Mr. Sohn Kee-Chung, a torch carrier of the 1988 Seoul Olympics, won the marathon in Berlin. But, alas, he had to swallow the humiliation of being saluted with the Japanese flag and national anthem.

Fifty-six years later, though, the very Sohn, now an octagenarian, witnessed a fellow Korean scoring a close yet stunning victory in the marathon and being showered with full-fledged honors of the Korean flag and its anthem. What a blessed and triumphant moment for both Korean athletes and their grateful country! What a happy commentary on the 25th Olympic Games!

We Korean-Americans proudly take this opportunity to salute those two world-class athletes.

REPETITIVE STRESS DOESN'T END AT THE WORKPLACE
Business Week, August 31, 1992

Readers Report

FIRST, LET'S ABSORB THE IMMIGRANTS WE'VE GOT

How many people can the U.S. accommodate before it finds itself, like China, in a situation where it is forced to try draconian methods to reduce its population? ("The Immigrants," Cover Story, July 13). In California, the population is now over 30 million; 50 million by the year 2000 has been predicted. Half of this growth has been attributed to immigrants. Population growth is the great enemy of the environment (clogged freeways, smoggy skies, inadequate water supplies, etc.).

As the son of immigrant parents, I have hesitated to advocate severe limits on immigration. Now, however, I recognize that what I owe my children outweighs my debt to my father's memory. We must stabilize our own population before opening the gates.

L. E. Sacks
Berkeley, Calif.

The tragedy is that by substantially reducing and enforcing immigration levels we could reduce social tensions and costs, more effectively assimilate the legal immigrants who are here, and begin to address the training, employment, and other issues that affect our own unskilled workers. We might even be more willing as a nation to encourage trade and aid that Third World countries need to offer opportunities to their own nationals.

George B. High
Executive Director
Center for Immigration Studies
Washington

REPETITIVE STRESS DOESN'T END AT THE WORKPLACE

In reference to your article "Repetitive stress: The pain has just begun" (Legal Affairs, July 13), the whole issue of repetitive strain injuries, or RSIs, appears to be far more complex than the legal profession attempts to make it. So many different factors are implicated or intertwined—medical, occupational, avocational, and genetical. Avocational or recreational activities outside of the job are just as important as vocational factors because RSIs are just as commonly encountered in recreational activities, such as bicycling, gardening, sewing, crocheting, knitting, baking, etc.

According to a recent Mayo Clinic report (June, 1992), one of the most frequently listed occupations of patients with carpal tunnel syndrome (CTS), in Rochester, Minn. (1961 through 1980), is homemaker (302 of 1,016), followed by retired persons. Surprisingly enough, female gender with use of oral contraceptives is reported to be the strongest of risk factors. To make matters worse, heredity or familial cases of CTS are now being reported increasingly.

Thus, the complexity of RSIs dictates a more thorough assessment of each case from the medical, vocational, avocational, and genetical standpoints. Otherwise, ergonomics and workplace modifications may only play a limited role as a preventive measure.

Chansoo Kim, M. D.
Physiatrist
Diplomate, American Board of
Physical Medicine & Rehabilitation
Springfield, Ill.

SMART SELLERS, SAVVY SAMARITANS

I read with great interest "Smart Selling" (Cover Story, Aug. 3). I watched with great anticipation to see W. Edwards Deming's name. But never once was the designer of these ideas mentioned. Do only the Japanese give credit where credit is due? Dr. Deming was teaching these ideas in the 1950s, but only the Japanese were listening. Shame!

Steven F. Marzorati
Rockford, Ill.

As a dedicated customer of Home Depot Inc., I read your cover story with interest. While Home Depot is savvy about its approach to selling to the do-it-yourself market, there is another dimension. Home Depot recognizes that it is an integral part of the greater community and takes that role as "corporate citizen" very seriously. About a year ago, a woman in the community lost her uninsured home and her teenage son to

BUSINESS WEEK
AUGUST 31, 1992 **3281
ISSN 0007-7135

Published weekly except for one issue in January, by McGraw-Hill Inc. Founder James H. McGraw (1860-1948). Executive, Editorial, Circulation, and Advertising Offices: McGraw-Hill Building, 1221 Avenue of the Americas, New York, N.Y. 10020. Telephone: (212) 512-2000. Domestic Telex: 12-7960; International Telex 232965; Cable McGraw-Hill New York; TWX: 710-581-1879. U.S. subscription rate $44.95 per year; 2 years, $74.95; 3 years, $99.90. Single copies, $2.75. Write for rates in other countries. Business Week Subscriber Services: 1-800-635-1200.

European Circulation Center, McGraw-Hill House, Maidenhead, Berks, England. Telephone (0628) 23431; Telex: 848840. Postmaster: Please send address changes to BUSINESS WEEK, P.O. Box 506, Hightstown, N.J. 08520. Second-class postage paid at New York, N.Y., and at additional mailing offices. Postage paid at Montreal, P.Q. Registration Number 9019. Registered for GST as McGraw-Hill Inc. GST #R123075673. Copyright ° 1992 by McGraw-Hill Inc. All rights reserved. Title registered in U.S. Patent Office.

Officers of McGraw-Hill Inc.: Joseph L. Dionne, Chairman, President and Chief Executive Officer; Robert N. Landes, Executive Vice President, General Counsel, and Secretary; Harold W. McGraw, III, Executive Vice President; Frank D. Penglase, Senior Vice President, Treasury Operations.

42

IT'S A COMPETITIVE
MARKET ECONOMY

(Chicago Tribune, October 22, 1992)

The Tribune's "The Daily Trouble" by Barbara Mahany (10/20/92) dwells on bare-knuckle competition among the three Korean-language Dailies in Chicago.

Much as I hate to say, I can't help but question the writer's ulterior motive. What's happening in the Korean community with their Korean-language newspapers should in no way be considered as unique or singular. Rather, it has to be viewed as a microcosm of our free enterprise system.

A case in point is our ailing airline industry. They have been fiercely waging a fare war. Some of them have already gone belly-up and others are thrown for a loop. Accusations fly around that big airlines rely on dirty tactics to push the weak and small over the cliff.

This is exactly what the business of America is all about. After all, free and competitive market economy determines success or failure of our businesses, whether small or big.

FIRST CIVILIAN LEADER
IN KOREA SINCE 1961

(The State Journal-Register, December 28, 1992)

Korea stands poised to usher in a new era of democracy with the recent election of a civilian leader as its president for the first time since 1961. Indeed, the road to democracy has been painfully long and tortuous, often punctuated by outbreaks of violence and outright vote fraud.

Unlike the previous elections, the 1992 Korean presidential election, held just a week before Christmas, was reported to be the freest ever. The Korean people have spoken loud and clear. The losing candidate conceded his defeat gracefully to President-elect Kim Young Sam, which is widely perceived as a rare commodity in Korean politics.

It now appears that Korea's nascent democracy has taken roots in its soil with a promising future to prosper and flourish over time. We've got to hand it to the Korean government and people as well.

We just hope that this watershed event will help propel South Korea toward peaceful reunification of their divided country.

LONG LIVE LINCOLN!

(Illinois Times, February 18, 1993)

Bob Sampson's Guestwork "The Untouchable" (see IT, February 12, 1993) leaves a bad taste in my mouth. Granted, everyone is entitled to his/her opinion. Yet Mr. Sampson's view of the Great Emancipator simply amounts to an academic exercise in futility.

One can hardly think of a political figure in the world's history whose life has been more intensely scrutinized and researched than Abe Lincoln, our sixteenth president. No aspect of his life escapes unscathed from our vetting process by a multitude of historians worldwide for well over a century.

Being a physician, I might add that Lincoln was even born genetically handicapped; it is no longer an idle speculation that Lincoln might have inherited Marfan's Syndrome. Worse yet, he is now suspected to have been a possible gene carrier of another devastating hereditary disease, which is called spino-cerebellar ataxia. Warts and all, Abe Lincoln had the strength to endure and triumph over the insurmountable obstacles in his way.

He will remain immortal not only in American history, but in the history of the world. Lincoln's legacy is so universal that even in the Far East, you hear schoolchildren fondly recite Lincoln's Gettysburg Address. Would this ever be attributed to "the cult of Lincoln" Bob Sampson is referring to? I think not. "Lincoln belongs to the ages." Also, he belongs to all people of all races.

On his 184th birthday, may the Lincoln legacy live on!

MENISCAL TEARS
Orthopaedic Review, March 1993

Comment & Response

To the Editor:

The Patient Guide on *Meniscal Tears*[1] in the November 1992 issue of *Orthopaedic Review* would have been an excellent piece of information for lay people were it not for one somewhat misleading point. Under the section discussing postsurgical care and rehabilitation of meniscal tears, the Patient Guide states that "a physical therapist might be recommended to design a program that will be best suited for the individual patient." I cannot help but view this statement with grave concern.

It is not a physical therapist but a physician who should design the most appropriate program for his or her patient. Certainly this is not to detract from or in any way slight the profession of physical therapy; I work very closely with physical therapists and value their service. However, a physical therapist only administers a therapeutic program specifically directed or outlined by the referring physician.

Chansoo Kim, MD
Springfield, Illinois

REFERENCE

1. Meniscal Tears. *Orthop Rev* 1992;21:1363–1364.

IT'S ABILITY THAT COUNTS

(Illinois Times, May 20, 1993)

As a specialist of rehabilitation medicine, I'd like to weigh in with my comments on "Future Block." (See IT, may 12, 1993). First, I congratulate the author on his timely and provocative article.

However, I am of the opinion that sheltered workshops and supported employment are two different programs and that they have each distinct roles to play in placement of workers with disabilities. No question that some of vocational trainees can and should be moved progressively from sheltered workshop settings to supported employment.

Unfortunately, very few people know that the University of Illinois at Champaign-Urbana deserves credit for being the first institution of higher learning in the nation to have enrolled students with disabilities even in the early 1960s. Illinoisans can justifiably take pride in the fact that their prestigious state university has been in the forefront. Some of our prominent state workers with disabilities are also graduates of the University of Illinois. Believe me, nothing gives me more pleasure than to see one of my former patients practice law as an attorney in town despite the severity of his disability. After all, it is ability that counts, not disability.

The Americans with Disabilities Act (ADA) is now the law of the land. Having been signed by former-President Bush in July 1990, it is often hailed as the most comprehensive legislation of its kind, and its historical significance is comparable with the Civil Rights Act of 1964.

Much to our delight, DORS (the Illinois Department of Rehabilitation Services) sets their sights on full implementation of ADA's employment provisions.

A short trip to Asia or Europe is more than enough to convince us that no other nation has come this far in creating a barrier-free and non-discriminatory society for persons with disabilities.

SECOND DOCTOR TELLS CONCERNS ABOUT ADS

(The State Journal-Register, May 23, 1993)

Dr. Irving S. Rossoff, megaditto from one of your colleagues in Springfield. I can't agree with you more. Please rest assured that you are speaking for the majority of physicians in central Illinois when you say you get annoyed by SIU Medical School's recent advertising blitz.

I myself have been in medical practice for only 30 years altogether, but it still irks me whenever I happen to tune in to the medical school's ballyhooing. Perhaps I am too old-fashioned or unsophisticated to comprehend the "all-important" role of ADS in today's medical practice.

Being a state institution, SIU Medical School, with its heavy promotional drive, might give the public the perception of unfair competition over the medical community. I sure realize that SIU PR Ads are sponsored and funded by a private foundation.

However, I believe that name recognition, like anything else, should be earned over time, not purchased by means of media. Instead, the money earmarked for commercial ads could be put to use for other worthwhile purposes such as accepting more indigent patients for their care, funding the research project or upgrading the medical school facility.

Any of these projects would go a long way toward making SIU a first-class medical school. Another strong argument against advertising by health care providers can be found in the public outcry for control of the skyrocketing health care costs.

For the past 20 years, much to its credit, SIU Medical School has grown by leaps and bounds. We hope to see the day when patients will flock to Springfield from overseas to seek top-notch care at SIU Medical School.

SHAVE AND A HAIRCUT . . . !

(AARP, May, 1993 Vol. 34, No. 5)

Susan L. Crowley's article, "The World According to Koop" (March Bulletin), reminds me of George Burns, who once said, "too bad the only people who know how to run the country are busy driving cabs and cutting hair."

In view of the urgency of the healthcare reform issue which confronts the nation, it is indeed too bad that people like Dr. C. Everett Koop, former U.S. surgeon general, are kept outside the Washington beltway.

SAY 'NO, THANKS'

(Chicago Tribune, June 7, 1993)

Chicago City Council clearly shows shallowness in its flippant decision to designate Lawrence Avenue in Albany Park as Seoul Drive. Apparently the move was taken to honor the Korean Community for its unique contribution to the revitalization of the neighborhood.

Regardless of its good intentions, the City Council, it is feared, unwittingly may play one ethnic group against another, thereby triggering racial tensions for a "turf" in a cosmopolitan city as ethnically diverse as Chicago.

Yet, there is no denying that some of the Korean entrepreneurs have turned the once ghost town into a booming business district. I say more power to them. There is nothing more gratifying than the honor of recognition in itself.

The Korean community should have been mature enough to gracefully turn down the controversial street sign. Anyway, what's in a name?

TO COMFORT ALWAYS

(Illinois Times, June 17, 1993)

Recently, the First Lady chided the medical profession in public for "price-gouging, cost-shifting, and unconscionable profiteering." Now, it is the dean of the SIU medical school who stigmatizes some physicians as "dollar-oriented," "Porsche-driving," and "lifestyle-intensive" (see "The Future of Medicine," IT, June 10, 1993). Believe me, I am neither a Porsche driver, nor do I drive a Mercedes Benz, for that matter.

First of all, what kind of life-style one chooses for oneself should be nobody else's business. What's more, a physician's life-style has got nothing to do with the ever-escalating health-care costs in the U.S.

How ironic it is that SIU School of Medicine serves as a magnet for so many super-specialists brought to town over the past twenty years, thus contributing in large measure to the elevated standards of healthcare in Springfield and, at the same time, driving its costs much higher for residents. Also, it is none other than SIU medical school that has run its aggressive promotional drive on TV and radio. How could one dare say that they are not business-motivated, if not money-oriented. Whose lifestyles are they seeking to enhance, medical students' or their faculty's? More than anything else, bigotry has no place in medicine.

Physicians in the real world have to pay higher malpractice premiums each year, (and now face) the stark reality of "economic credentialing" as blatantly practiced at most hospitals in the nation. We are much concerned about and deeply troubled by the soaring healthcare costs which, if left to its own device, will ultimately hurt every one of us.

On the other hand, the medical profession alone can't be singled out for the current plight of our health delivery system. There is more than enough blame to go around. That is, malpractice (litigation) with defensive medicine, high technology, demographic changes with the graying of America, super-specialization of medicine, etc.

Medical profession-bashing aside, it is well known that U.S. has the most expensive healthcare in the world. What is not well known is that we also have by far the best healthcare in the world, thanks to availability of advanced technology, highly specialized medicine, and experts with unsurpassed skills.

For the vast majority of physicians, however, "to cure sometimes, to relieve often, to comfort always" will remain the motto of their medical practice, and it should.

UH, MAYBE THAT SHOULD
HAVE BEEN 'ULTIMATE'

(Illinois Times, June 29, 1993)

It seems that argots or jargons are crawling out of the woodwork. It's often so confusing and outright daunting, particularly to the foreign-born, to even try to catch up with them, let alone comprehend their meanings.

I am referring to your recent articles in IT (6/24/93) where "SSU President Naomi Lynn is Playing the Penultimate Diplomat." What in Sam's hill is meant by the penultimate diplomat? Webster's New World Dictionary defines the word penultimate as next to the last.

Perhaps you can enlighten me on this enigmatic word.

Footnote:

Penultimate—One of the most confusable and misused English words.

A naval commander stoutly defended Star Wars as being both scientifically feasible and strategically desirable. He concluded, "In Star Wars, America has finally come up with the penultimate defense system!"

But penultimate doesn't mean the absolute ultimate (Can anything be more ultimate?) Derived from Latin, Paene, "almost", and Ultimus, "last", penultimate means 'next to last'.

Thinking that pen—was an intensifier rather than a qualifier, our naval commander ended up saying the opposite of what he meant. The last thing we want is a penultimate defense system against nuclear weapons.

BOB DRYSDALE
GOLF TOURNAMENT

(The State Journal-Register, July 26, 1993)

The State Journal Register's Bob Drysdale Golf Tournament holds a special place in our hearts. At this time of year, we make it our habit to follow closely the young people's famed golf tourney, the outcome of which always attracts our attention in the paper.

I fondly recall taking my son to the Bergen Park ten years ago for his final match in the 13-under Division. We still cherish very much the happy memory of Richard's capturing the championship title in 1983.

Much to our chagrin, however, we couldn't find his name in the published roster of the past Drysdale champions from 1937 to 1993, (State Journal-Register, July 24, 1993).

We feel somewhat slighted by your complete and blatant omission of his name, and we can't help but wonder if you have committed this obvious blunder accidentally on purpose, because we noticed the same error in the past.

I am merely bringing this up in order that the Drysdale's historical record may be set straight once and for all. I strongly believe credit should be given where credit is due.

At Bergen Park

Richard Kim of Springfield and Bryan Graiff of Litchfield will play for the 13-and-under title with an 18-hole round scheduled for 8 a.m. today.

in Drysdale

Springfield's Richard Kim won the 13-under division at Bergen Park. Story is on page 21.

The State Journal-Register, Springfield, Illinois   Friday, June 17, 1983   Page 21

Kim captures 13-under Drysdale meet at Bergen

Springfield's Richard Kim parred the No. 6 hole at Bergen Park Thursday to take a 3-and-2 win over Litchfield's Bryan Graiff for the 13-and-under championship of the State Journal-Register Bob Drysdale Golf Tournament.

Kim took an early lead in the 18-hole title match, winning the third hole with a bogey 5. Graiff pulled even on No. 4, but Kim went 2-up by parring No. 7 and bogeying No. 9.

Graiff got back to 1-down by parring No. 1, but Kim then parred Nos. 2 and 4 to go 3-up. After Graiff parred No. 5 to get back to 2-down, Kim parred Nos. 6 and 7 to close out the match.

Six other championships were decided at Bergen Thursday. In the consolation flight, Litchfield's Matt Buske defeated Jacksonville's Jay Davis 2-and-1. In the first flight, Springfield's Dennis Pfeffer beat Springfield's Jon McCormick 2-and-1.

Other flight winners were Petersburg's Greg Clary 5-and-4 over Springfield's Scott Teague in the second; Springfield's Tim Mattsson 4-and-3 over Springfield's Jason Clark in the third; Springfield's David Grady 3-and-2 over Springfield's Kirk Anderson in the fourth, and Springfield's Tim Nicoud 2-and-1 over Springfield's Keith Driver in the fifth.

PAST CHAMPIONS ROSTERS

Saturday, July 24, 1993
The State Journal-Register

Drysdale data

PAST CHAMPIONS

1937 — Bud Hemphill, Carlinville
1938 — Don Street, Rushville
1939 — Don Street, Rushville
1940 — Don Street, Rushville
1941 — Jack Coyle, Springfield
1942 — Jack Coyle, Springfield
1943 — Kelly Graham, Springfield
1944 — Bob Starbody, Decatur
1945 — Don Fairfield, Jacksonville
1946 — Don Fairfield, Jacksonville
1947 — Don Fairfield, Jacksonville
1948 — Norm Rodier, Springfield
1949 — Norm Rodier, Springfield
1950 — No tournament, polio quarantine
1951 — Bob Rovin, Springfield
1952 — Jerry Meidel, Springfield
1953 — Cullen Patton, Springfield
1954 — Pete Beardsley, Springfield
1955 — Frank Sparks, Springfield
1956 — Larry Wallden, Peoria
1957 — Tommy Farrell, Jacksonville
1958 — Bob Bradley, Jacksonville
1959 — Joe Ashcraft, Rushville
1960 — Lynn Morrison, Springfield
1961 — Doug Carson, Springfield
1962 — Doug Carson, Springfield
1963 — Doug Carson, Springfield
1964 — Dick Stephens, Rushville
1965 — Ray Stotler, Carlinville
1966 — Paul Werkman, Lincoln
1967 — Joe Thompson, Sullivan
1968 — Phil Whitler, Girard
1969 — Don Dray, Pekin
1970 — Phil Whitler, Girard
x-1971 — J.D. Evans, Jacksonville
1972 — Scott Kiriakos, Springfield
1973 — Ron Beck, Decatur
1974 — Ray Goodman, Decatur
1975 — Tom Ferlmann, Peoria
1976 — Tom Ferlmann, Peoria
1977 — Pat Venker, Bloomington
1978 — Jim Tureskis, Springfield
1979 — Doug Williams, Springfield
1980 — Mark Young, Petersburg
1981 — Sam Beck, Decatur
1982 — Rick Poggi, Springfield (Al Bergen — Mike Mathiot, Springfield).
1983 — Paul Baisler, Springfield (Al Bergen — Jay Davis, Jacksonville).
1984 — Kevin Fry, Petersburg
1985 — Matt Dudley, Chatham
1986 — Mike Mathiot, Springfield (Al Bergen — Rob Hoskins, Springfield).

GOLF

Past Drysdale champions

1937 — Bud Hemphill, Carlinville
1938 — Don Street, Rushville
1939 — Don Street, Rushville
1940 — Don Street, Rushville
1941 — Jack Coyle, Springfield
1942 — Jack Coyle, Springfield
1943 — Kelly Graham, Springfield
1944 — Bob Starbody, Decatur
1945 — Don Fairfield, Jacksonville
1946 — Don Fairfield, Jacksonville
1947 — Don Fairfield, Jacksonville
1948 — Norm Rodier, Springfield
1949 — Norm Rodier, Springfield
1950 — No tournament, polio quarantine
1951 — Bob Rovin, Springfield
1952 — Jerry Meidel, Springfield
1953 — Cullen Patton, Springfield
1954 — Pete Beardsley, Springfield
1955 — Frank Sparks, Springfield
1956 — Larry Walden, Peoria
1957 — Tommy Farrell, Jacksonville
1958 — Bob Bradley, Jacksonville
1959 — Joe Ashcraft, Rushville
1960 — Lynn Morrison, Springfield
1961 — Doug Carson, Springfield
1962 — Doug Carson, Springfield
1963 — Doug Carson, Springfield
1964 — Dick Stephens, Rushville
1965 — Ray Slottler, Carlinville
1966 — Paul Werkman, Lincoln
1967 — Joe Thompson, Sullivan
1968 — Phil Whitler, Girard
1969 — Don Dray, Pekin
1970 — Phil Whitler, Girard
x-1971 — J.D. Evans, Jacksonville
1972 — Scott Kriakos, Springfield
1973 — Ron Beck, Decatur
1974 — Ray Goodman, Decatur
1975 — Tom Ferlmann, Peoria
1976 — Tom Ferlmann, Peoria
1977 — Pat Venker, Bloomington
1978 — Jim Tureskis, Springfield
1979 — Doug Williams, Springfield
1980 — Mark Young, Petersburg
1981 — Sam Beck, Decatur
1982 — Rick Pogol, Springfield (Al Bergen
— Mike Malhiot, Springfield).
1983 — Paul Balser, Springfield (Al Bergen — Jay Davis, Jacksonville).
1984 — Kevin Fry, Petersburg (Al Bergen — ????)
1985 — Matt Dudley, Chatham (Al Bergen — Chad Sprecher, Chatham)
1986 — Mike Malhiot, Springfield (Al Bergen — Rob Hoskins, Springfield).
1987 — Jay Davis, Jacksonville (Al Bergen —, Jeff Call, Springfield).
1988 — T.J. Carroll, Petersburg (Al Bergen — Jeff Roper, Litchfield).
1989 — T.J. Carroll, Petersburg (Al Bergen — Kevin Corn, Greenville).
1990 — Bobby Sims, Jacksonville (Al Bergen — Keith Ward, Jacksonville).
1991 — Scott Glisson, Springfield (Al Bergen — Doyle Moffit, Florissant, Mo.)
y-1992 — Al Bunn: Boys — Cory Wells, Rochester; Girls — Kourtney Mulcahy, Springfield.
Al Bergen: Boys — Barclay Brown, Staunton. Girls — Laura Patrick, Rochester.
1993 — Al Bunn: Boys: — Cory Wells, Rochester; Girls — Laura Patrick, Rochester.
Al Bergen: Boys — Nick Nell, Jacksonville; Girls — Eileen Myer, Edwardsville.
x-Tourney split into 13-under and 14-17 age groups.
y-First year for separate girls' divisions

Bobby Nichols 73-70—143 +1
Randy Glover 73-70—143 +1
Marlon Heck 72-71—143 +1
Dick Goetz 71-72—143 +1
Simon Hobday 69-74—143 +1
Joe Jimenez 72-72—144 +2
Bob Dickson 71-73—144 +2
Fred Ruiz 69-75—144 +2
Bob Carson 74-71—145 +3
Jim Dent 70-72—145 +3
Babe Hiskey 72-73—145 +3
Gay Brewer 72-73—145 +3
Mike Joyce 72-73—145 +3
Randy Petri 72-73—145 +3
Rives McBee 70-75—145 +3
Homero Blancas 70-75—145 +3
Orville Moody 69-76—145 +3
Jesse Vaughn 73-73—146 +4
Mike Fetchick 73-73—146 +4
George Archer 72-74—146 +4
Bob Panasik 71-75—146 +4
Miller Barber 70-76—146 +4
Dick Rhyan 70-76—146 +4
Robert Gaona 77-70—147 +5
Rod Curl 75-72—147 +5
Don Bies 74-73—147 +5
Terry Dill 72-75—147 +5
Billy Maxwell 75-73—148 +6
Charlie Owens 74-74—148 +6
John Paul Cain 72-76—148 +6
Richard Bassett 71-77—148 +6
Dick Hendrickson 71-77—148 +6
Ben Smith 69-79—148 +6
Denny Spencer 77-72—149 +7
Bob Goalby 76-73—149 +7
Dick Lotz 74-75—149 +7
Jerry Barber 74-75—149 +7
Harry Toscano 72-77—149 +7
Gene Littler 70-79—149 +7
Howie Johnson 72-78—150 +8
Dick Plummer 76-75—151 +9
Dow Finsterwald 75-76—151 +9
Jack Fleck 74-77—151 +9
Bruce Crampton 74-77—151 +9
Dick James 76-76—152 +10
Bob Rosburg 81-72—153 +11
Doug Ford 80-74—154 +12
Butch Leal 81-77—158 +16

July 11, 1994

Dear Mr. Clarke:

This letter is self-explanatory because I am sending copies of all pertinent correspondence to you. As far as I am concerned, I have to state flat out that this case represents nothing but racism with arrogance, which I cannot stand any longer.

In my letter to the editor on June 26, 1993, in which I enclosed your State Journal-Register newspaper article on my son, who won the 13-under Drysdale Tournament Championship on June 17, 1983, I asked for correction and apparently they have never taken care of it, nor have I had any official response from the State Journal-Register to date. I am telling you now that we are deeply hurt beyond words. Perhaps this is the last straw that broke the camel's back.

I don't need any apology from the State Journal-Register or from you, but I do need your explanation as to why my son's name, which may sound foreign to you, was omitted and why, in your opinion, he does not deserve to be on the list of the Drysdale Championship Roster as published on Sunday.

This morning, I spoke to Mr. Jim Ruppert, one of the State Journal-Register sports editors, and he indicated there was no winner recorded in the 1983 13-under Drysdale Championship Roster.

Very truly yours,

Chansoo Kim, M.D.

(Sports Editor's Response, July 12, 1993)

The State Journal-Register

ONE COPLEY PLAZA   POST OFFICE BOX 219   SPRINGFIELD, ILLINOIS 62705-0219   (217) 788-1300

July 12, 1993

Dr. Chansoo Kim
39 Glen Eagle Dr.
Springfield, IL. 62704

Dear Dr. Kim,

Just to repeat the sentiment I expressed on the telephone during our July 11, 1994, conversation, apologies to you and your son, Richard Kim, for the mistake The State Journal-Register made in its July 10 listing of past Drysdale Junior Golf champions.

As noted in the July 12 editions of The State Journal-Register, we have corrected our error and now have Richard Kim listed as the winner of the 1983 Drysdale title, Bergen Park division. In originally recording the information, one of our reporters mistakenly listed 1984 Bergen winner Jay Davis as the 1983 winner, and we regret the error. We also regret not clearing up the mistake one year ago, when you brought it to our attention.

Please feel free to contact me at The State Journal-Register if I can be of any further assistance to you.

Respectfully,

Jim Ruppert
Sports Editor

Correspondence from John P. Clarke, Publisher of State
Journal-Register July 13, 1994

JOHN P. CLARKE
PUBLISHER
ONE COPLEY PLAZA   POST OFFICE BOX 219   SPRINGFIELD, ILLINOIS 62705-0219   (217) 788-1500

Our 163rd Year
July 13, 1994

Chansoo Kim, M.D.
619 South Fourth Street
Springfield, IL 62703

Dear Dr. Kim:

I thank you for your recent letter concerning an error which recently
appeared in our newspaper in a listing of past champions of the State
Journal-Register Drysdale Golf Tournament.

While you don't ask for an apology, I must nevertheless extend our
apologies to you and your son for our repeated error. Unfortunately, I am
unable to offer any explanation as to why your son's name did not appear
as the 1983 13-and-under tournament champion. Unfortunately, I have
been unable to obtain a satisfactory explanation as to how we could repeat
the same error in 1994 that we made in 1993 after the matter was brought
to our attention last year.

I can, however, offer you full assurances that your son's race or national
origin had nothing to do with the problem. At the same time, I offer to you
our full assurances that this error will not reoccur when the listing of prior
Drysdale champions is published next year prior to the 1995 tournament.

Once again, I appreciate your bringing this matter to my attention and hope
that this letter represents some measure of satisfaction to you.

Sincerely,

cc: Steve Fagan
     Patrick Coburn
     Jim Ruppert

dw

63

PRAISES EDITORIAL ABOUT BUREAUCRACY

(The State Journal-Register, October 3, 1993)

The State Journal Register editorial of Sept. 21 deserves our unsparing applause for its poignant yet timely comment on bloated bureaucracy.

If one just doesn't practice what one preaches, their message is bound to be hollow and rhetorical. These two apt words—hypocritical and disingenuous—have found their rightful place in the editorial. And they say it all, loud and clear.

Talk is always cheap. What we do need most is action now rather than a theatrical gesture.

The public is well served by your excellent editorial.

SALE OF GACY ARTWORK SICKENING SITUATION

(The State Journal-Register, October 24, 1993)

As the popular saying goes, "It takes all kinds of people to make a world." Indeed, how true it is!

I am specifically referring to the appalling news that John W. Gacy, the most heinous serial killer, attempted to sell off his "artwork" and even some of his personal belongings while on death row.

What is no less frightening is the fact that some people went head over heels to purchase his ghoulish paintings. Artwork, my foot! I wouldn't touch them with a 10-foot pole. Who on earth would dare to be haunted by the innocent victims the demoniac murdered in cold blood?

This grotesque incident makes me wonder whether we are living in a sick world, or we are just a bunch of sick people.

COLLEGE COP-OUT

(Illinois Times, November 11, 1993)

According to Illinois Board of Higher Education (IBHE), ever-increasing enrollment of minority students the past few years at Illinois colleges and universities is inversely proportional to their retention rates. This disconcerting trend visible among minority groups obviously causes state officials to frantically look for what is really at fault with higher education.

Could you ever imagine "some African-American students experiencing culture shock when they come to predominantly white schools?" It is rather outlandish that, of all other plausible causes, "culture shock" should be singled out as the villain for their high failure ratio. What a knee slapper!

If you will, take up the case of foreign students who flock to U.S. campuses in droves every fall. Don't they suffer literally from the triple whammy of culture shock, language barriers and higher tuition? Any wonder they all manage to successfully complete their education even when the odds are clearly stacked against them.

What's more, it is a well-known fact that a greater number of foreign graduate students are currently being enrolled in postgraduate doctoral programs across the country.

No matter how you slice it, the façade of "culture shock 101" sure sounds like a cop-out.

CLINTON BACKS OFF FIRM STAND ON NORTH KOREA

(The State Journal-Register, December 7, 1993)

While Uncle Sam is being wrapped up in "nation-building" missions in Somalia and Haiti, the back burner issue of North Korea's nuclear weapons program begins to raise its ugly head.

Amid ominous signs of an impending crisis on the Korean peninsula, the Clinton administration boldly took a firm line with the North Koreans just a few weeks ago, issuing a warning in no uncertain terms that "our patience is not unlimited," and "Pyongyang must not be allowed to develop a nuclear bomb."

Now, this one-night stand of firmness is doing a 180-degree turn. As reported, the new official U.S. move would instead reward North Korea with a comprehensive package of incentives: a) cancellation of annual U.S.-South Korean military exercises (Team Spirit); b) another "endless" round of high-level talks with North Korea; c) a promise of economic aid; d) ultimately, possible diplomatic relations between Washington and Pyongyang—all of these goodies in exchange for suspension of their nuclear project and cooperation with U.N. inspection of their clandestine nuclear sites.

This about-face in U.S. policy sends at best a mixed signal and inevitably helps support the notion that Washington is showing the white feather to the Communists in North Korea. The North's rogue dictator would jump at the opportunity to play their favorite stalling games with U.N. inspection teams.

Time is of essence and it is on their side. With passage of time, nuclear dangers in the Far Eastern region will only grow. It is feared that Mr. Clinton finally "opens door" for a future darker than ever.

CLINTON FOREIGN POLICY UNDER ATTACK

(The State Journal-Register, January 5, 1994)

Your Dec. 13 editorial obviously reminds us of a fairy tale. You indicated that somehow the "full-blown crisis" with North Korea could be resolved with a happy ending. How naïve it is!

Now, we are rather stunned to learn of the new U.S. position that "North Korea can have old nuclear bombs but not new ones." A recent salvo of unmistakable warnings issued to North Korea by the Clinton administration have all turned out to be idle threats. The penetrating question is, does the Clinton administration ever mean what they say? Or, do they say what they mean?

Which naturally brings to mind the misguided U.S. policy in Somalia whereby our 18 young and brave soldiers were killed early in October during the raid to capture Samali warlord Mohammed Farah Aidid.

I dare challenge anybody to top this cockamamie shift in U.S. foreign policy: barely two months following the massacre, American soldiers were being used again, this time to escort the same villain to the Mogadishu airport and fly him on a U.S. plane for "peace talks."

Then, would it be way out of line or even far-fetched to extrapolate that one of these days, heinous dictator Kim Il Sung or his heir Kim

Jong Il will be flown to Washington for direct talks with President Clinton?

Trying to reach out to the unreachable and reason with the unreasonable is indeed noble, but it is utter folly in the real world. One blunder here, another blunder there, and it will soon add up to a major crisis for which we are now headed.

POLITICAL CORRECTNESS RUN AMOK

(The State Journal-Register, February 1, 1994)

Political correctness (PC) has become such a rage in our society that we need to have a PC dictionary, if any, handy on our desk alongside the Webster's English Dictionary.

These days, it is not unusual to come across such equivocal phrases as "physically and socially or mentally challenged," or "differently abled" in reference to the disabled. To top it off, now the tongue-in-cheek expression, "vertically challenged" crops up for short people.

Apparently, this vicious PC virus (mind you, not personal computer) has now infected Britain, our closest ally across the Atlantic. Could you imagine that recently, a head school teacher there refused to let her students see the ballet "Romeo and Juliet," on the grounds that it was "blatantly heterosexual." Sensitivity to certain segments of our society is one thing, and outright censorship is another thing.

Please save our good old English language. It has been taking real bad beatings from the political correctness movement run amok. Before we know it, some of our favorite English words and expressions will be altogether banished from the English language. Just to name some of the potential victims, they are: Indian summer, honest injun, paleface, redskin, handyman, mankind, Welsh, Dutch treat and Dutch uncle, etc.

Are we going to have the Orwellian style thought police, or are we doomed to be mealy-mouthed?

Political correctness, if relentlessly and mercilessly pushed, may fly in the face of the First Amendment of the Constitution.

PLENTY OF BEDS

(Illinois Times, February 10, 1994)

While discussing drastic changes under managed care with Clinton's health care reform, Dr. Carl Getto, Dean of S.I.U. Medical School, erroneously put Springfield's hospital bed capacity at 800 to 1,000 (see "Managed care means big changes here," IT, January 27, 1994).

The fact of the matter is, his guesstimate is way below the actual number of beds available in all three community hospitals. Just to set the record straight, St. John's Hospital has well over 700 beds; Memorial Medical Center, over 550 beds; Doctors Hospital, 177 beds.

Currently, Springfield literally enjoys a glut of hospital beds—a mind-boggling sum of at least 1, 500 beds.

Perhaps Dr. Getto may have made this factual error because he is a newcomer in the medical community.

THE GULAG ON SAKHALIN ISLAND

(Chicago Tribune, February 22, 1994)

Amid a hue and cry over Serbian's ethnic cleansing, which now calls for U.N. airstrikes, there comes the shocking revelation that tens of thousands of poor souls have still been trapped alive in the frigid coal mines for over 50 years. That's precisely what's happening to the Koreans abandoned on Sakhalin Island as part of the Japanese war efforts. Largely due to the Japanese infamous cover-ups, the tragic plight of the Sakhalin Koreans remains to date concealed to the rest of the world.

For one thing, Japanese people are swift as an arrow to put out all kinds of gizmos on the world market, but they are lamentably slow as molasses to admit their past wrongs. Not too long ago, confronted with the disgraceful issue of "comfort women" as sex slaves during the war, the Japanese government initially deadpanned and then kept on stonewalling it, only to own up to their despicable involvement. We also remember too well Japan's tinkering with her ugly past history of naked aggression for "sanitization."

What Auschwitz and Dachau are to the six million Jews, Sakhalin is to the fifty thousand Koreans languishing for half a century on the "Isle of Tears."

It's high time that Tokyo should finally free their war prisoners from the Gulag, putting an end to their version of Apartheid for 700,000 Korean residents in Japan.

VANDALS WILL GET AWAY WITH SLAP ON THE WRIST

(The State Journal-Register, May 15, 1994)

On the heels of the notorious Michael Fay case, which has raised such a ruckus here and abroad, we can't help but feel utterly ashamed to hear of the despicable acts of rampant vandalism as reported in Elkhart, Ill., when the four Sangamon County young men smashed off the head and right arm of the hallowed "doughboy" statue during their three-week crime spree.

We have good news for these shameless thugs; they have committed their acts of vandalism here in America, not in Singapore, and they will most likely get away with a slap on the wrist. Our political and criminal justice system will see to it that no "harsh punishment" is being meted out to them. Under all circumstances, "the punishment will fit the crime."

Meanwhile, our hearts go out to Elkhart residents, who are trying to have the statue repaired by all means before Memorial Day.

Is it any wonder why the majority of Americans come out and say, "Michael Fay had it coming."

Critique

SOME CONVICTING MEN
BEFORE THEY'RE TRIED

(The State Journal-Register, May 23, 1994)

Dear Editor,

In regard to the so called "shameless thugs" in the Doughboy case, aren't people supposed to be innocent until proven guilty?

Who is to say which, if any, of these four young men actually did the physical damage to the Doughboy or may be guilty by association.

It seems to me some people already have them tried and guilty. I will base my opinions on facts, not hearsay.

Johnna C. McArdle
Springfield

DOUGHBOY COMES BACK TO ELKHART

(The State Journal-Register, April 26, 1995)

The village's favorite resident, a 1919 statue of a doughboy, rode into town Tuesday and was hoisted by crane back onto his pedestal overlooking the hamlet's main drag, nearly a year after vandals decapitated the World War I monument.

"Now we can look back on that side of the street again," said Gwen Rosenfeld, whose great-great grandfather John Shockey founded the village in 1819. "It was just sad going by there, knowing it was supposed to be there. It left an empty space in your heart."

Without notifying the village in advance, Arnold Monument Co. of Springfield, surprised residents Tuesday by returning the monument at 11 a.m.

A little more than a year ago, on March 29, 1994, the sleepy village of 475 awoke to find vandals had struck the landmark, knocking off its head and shattering the concrete gun and the right hand that held it for 75 years.

The town answered the battle call by rounding up a $1,000 reward for anyone with information about the crime.

Four teens from the Rochester and Springfield area eventually were convicted of the offense, as well as other charges of criminal damage in a vandalism spree that took place in Logan, Sangamon and Christian counties.

Village residents, still bristling from the vandalism and the fact that they have yet to see a penny of restitution from the four youths, will be keeping an eye on any suspicious activity around the doughboy, vowed Elkhart native Bill Cosby.

"We'll put out a dead or alive bounty on the next person who tries to mess with the doughboy," said Cosby, commander of the Elkhart American Legion.

Immediately after the vandalism, it was doubtful whether the doughboy would be put together again—after the village received a $3,000 repair estimate.

Village clerk Virgil Sprunger said it now appears the doughboy damage was covered by the village's insurance policy. But Rosenfeld said the community would have supported bringing the doughboy back, even if everyone had had to chip in.

"The reason that means so much to this town is there are still people living here that are listed (on the plaques at the base of the statue, listing war-time service,)" she said. "We're not a rich community, but there's loyalty (to the doughboy) among residents."

The doughboy statue, funded by the federal government, first came to town after World War I.

NORTH KOREAN GOAL

(Chicago Tribune, July 8, 1994)

In reference to what Robert T. Yeager opined in his letter (June 19), I categorically state that Mr. Yeager's got it all backwards, totally oblivious of North Korea's odious history—its naked aggression and relentless resort thereafter to abominable terrorism against Seoul.

If you recall, Pyongyang was "bombed into dust" during the Korean War, which dictator Kim Il Sung started 44 years ago with a blitzkrieg invasion into South Korea. Domination! Talk about it. North's renegade regime under the same old monomaniacal despot is now hellbent for nuclear buildup.

Despite "a lot of pressure from the Right to get tough with North Korea," President Clinton boldly offered to the Communists last fall what's considered "the most creative and comprehensive peace package yet." But they simply walked away from it.

Let's get real. Kim Il Sung still remains consumed with an insatiable desire to push his one and only agenda, which is unification of the Korean peninsula on his own political terms.

AFFECT VS. EFFECT

(Chicago Tribune, July 27, 1994)

Joan Beck's article, "Best thing Congress can do is slow down on health care issue" (7-24-94) couldn't be more timely, and it figuratively hits the nail on the head. She deserves high marks for such an articulate and lucid article on the most complex issue of health care reform that faces the nation.

Unfortunately, her incorrect use of the word 'effect' as in "figure out how it will effect us" is regrettable and can be the fly in the ointment. Granted, affect/effect are two of the most misused words, even among professional writers.

Footnote:

The verbs *affect* and *effect* produce important differences in meaning. Using *effect* in the sentence *The measures have been designed to effect savings* implies that the measures will cause new savings to come about. Using *affect* in the very similar sentence *These measures will affect savings* implies that the measures will cause a change in savings that have already been realized.

CLINTON HAS COME TO RESCUE OF N. KOREA

(The State Journal-Register, November 9, 1994)

The "historic" U.S.-North Korea accord finally signed in Geneva spells nothing but a potential disaster for Washington despite its disingenuous claims to the contrary.

For one thing, Uncle Sam literally gave the store away to Pyongyang, and the communists are just gloating over the diplomatic hat trick which they could pull off even at the time of their losing battle for survival.

The irony is that the Clinton administration has come to their rescue in the nick of time. Clinton's resuscitation kit for the North contains, among all others: a) a $4 billion modern, light-water nuclear reactor—mind you, at no cost to Pyongyang; b) $100 million worth of much-needed oil from the U.S. each year; c) five years' reprieve from U.N. inspection of the two clandestine, "off-limits" nuclear plants.

To top it off, they are also being rewarded with our diplomatic and economic ties and voluntary cancellation of the joint U.S.-South Korea military exercises (Team Spirit).

In return, we get only a signed piece of paper from the rogue Pyongyang regime in which they agree to stop producing more nuclear bombs and allow the U.N. to resume its inspection of their "existing" nuclear facilities.

To quote George Santayana, an American author of the early 20th century, "those who cannot remember the past are condemned to repeat it." Unfortunately, the specter of the North Korean deal may haunt Bill Clinton long after he has left office.

ALTERNATIVES LATEST IN POLITICAL CORRECTNESS

(American Medical News, November 21, 1994)

AMNews deserves high marks for the most timely and revealing article, "Beyond Allopathy." Indeed, it sheds some light on the future direction of our whole health care system.

What used to be quackery, they now call "alternative medicine" as opposed to "conventional medicine." Whether we like it or not, alternative medicine has finally taken its toehold in the field of health care delivery, thanks to the surging movement of political correctness and cultural diversity run amok.

Perhaps "alternative medicine" might as well be named "political medicine."

U. S. POSTAL SERVICE URGED TO ISSUE ITS COMMEMORATIVE STAMP

(The State Journal-Register, December 7, 1994)

The Japanese government's brazen protest against the pending issuance of a U.S. commemorative mushroom cloud stamp jolts us again with a grim reminder: Japan as a nation obviously is still unwilling or unable to accept the historic fact that the Pacific War started with their unprovoked attack on Pearl Harbor and ended four years later with their unconditional surrender only after the U.S. dropped nuclear bombs on Hiroshima and Nagasaki about 50 years ago.

Naturally, we are just outraged, to say the least, to see the Japanese always portray themselves as the victims of the war, while callously turning their backs on the barbaric atrocities the Rising Sun had visited upon the entire Far Eastern region under their tyrannical rule.

Painful as it may be, it is historically accurate that the nuclear bombs not only did hasten the end of the war, but saved a countless number of lives here and abroad from the ravages of the war.

We can't urge too strongly that the U.S. Postal service forge ahead with its original plan. Meanwhile, it is just our hope against hope that Japan finally rid herself of the ingrained delusion and come to grips with her past history of war crimes.

DO WE REALLY NEED A NEW ACCESS SYMBOL

(The Wall Street Journal, February 21, 1995)

In reference to the February 17th Wall Street Journal article, "Form + Function" by John Pierson, I am compelled to make the following comments.

First and foremost, the Department of Rehabilitation Services, State of Illinois, has been using as its official emblem exactly the same "open door" symbol as reportedly designed by Mr. Brendan Murphy. As one can readily see, DORS, for short, rhymes with the word "door," thus literally opening the door of opportunity to their clients with disabilities.

This might very well be the case of sheer coincidence, and I do not intend at all to impugn Mr. Murphy in any way, shape or form, with plagiarism or anything close to it. Rather, I thought that the public should be apprised of the fact that the "open door" symbol is not something new and has been in existence for years, and that the Illinois Department of Rehabilitation Services should be credited for its originality.

Secondly, as regards to the bold suggestion of replacing the current international access symbol with the proposed "universal open door," I am of the opinion that the time-honored handicapped sign is globally too popular to tinker with. As the old axiom goes, why fix it if it ain't broken?

SPEAKS IN DEFENSE OF
USE OF ATOMIC BOMB

(The State Journal-Register, February 23, 1995)

It is a sad commentary on the 50th anniversary that both the Smithsonian Institution and the U. S. Postal Service timidly became too weak-kneed to tell the historic event of the World War II like it is: the dropping of an atomic bomb on Hiroshima played a decisive role in bringing Japan to its knees with unconditional surrender.

Granted, the first nuclear bombs ever used in human history inflicted upon the Japanese devastating destruction beyond measure. Yet, the flip side is that they also saved countless human lives, here and abroad.

Let us not forget that President Truman, with his courageous stroke of no-nonsense action, had all at once liberated Korea and its surrounding region from the blood-dripping grip of Imperial Japan.

Here's something for history revisionists to think over: what if the U.S. had used an atomic bomb a year earlier, or better yet, in 1941, right after the Pearl Harbor attack. Then most of Japan's gruesome war crimes and atrocities, including biological warfare units and "comfort women," would have been aborted. As the saying goes, hindsight is always 20/20.

No matter how tragic or ugly it may be, let history be history. Again, "those who can't remember the past are condemned to repeat it."

AIDS AND GENOCIDE

(Illinois Times, March 9, 1995)

Acquired Immune Deficiency Syndrome is caused by HIV virus for which, to this date, there has been found no cure and from which no race is known to be immune, regardless of sex and age.

Despite the intensive medical researches feverishly carried out world-wide the past decade, AIDS infection is still spreading like wildfire, and the most dreadful disease is now called the plague of the century.

I am utterly speechless to read about what I would call the sheer delusion that "AIDS virus was genetically manufactured by Uncle Sam to target black people as a genocidal tool." That takes the cake! Nevertheless, no one in the medical community would give credence to such cooked-up "epidemic ideology." It's as sickening as it is asinine.

Nowhere is the specter of AIDS so keenly felt as in the medical profession. Some of the "high-risk" physicians are now advised to take out special insurance policy for "AIDS coverage only."

In the meantime, our time would be well spent if we stay focused on public education of AIDS prevention rather than scurry around with the disinformation. What you <u>don't</u> know <u>can</u> hurt you.

Critique

EARLY DIAGNOSIS

(Illinois Times, March 30-April 5, 1995)

To the Editor,

Dr. Chansoo Kim's rejection of the "asinine belief" that AIDS was manufactured at Fort Detrick by the U.S. Biowarfare Department as an ethnic weapon (see "Epidemic Ideology," *IT*, March 2, 1995) is presumably based on his total ignorance of the supporting documentation in the Congressional Record, in the *World Health Organization Bulletin*, and in the Military Review, to name only a few of the sources quoted by Black Liberation Radio and recorded in my book Media Matters. His assertion that "no one in the medical community" would give the belief credence reveals his equal ignorance of Dr. Alan Cantwell's books AIDS and *the Doctors of Death and Queer Blood*. He is presumably as ignorant of the work of Dr. Robert Strecker. I would have expected a medical doctor to do some research before making a diagnosis.

John Fiske
Madison, Wisconsin

ATTACK ON REPUBLICANS A 'PACK OF BLATANT LIES'

(The State Journal-Register, March 23, 1995)

The mainstream news media outlets and the Clinton administration join forces in their venomous, all-out attack against the Republican party's welfare reforms.

Nowadays, we get hit almost daily with a barrage of Dickensian horror stories about the school lunch program. "Newt, the scrooge, is taking away school lunches"; "our children are going to be malnourished, starved and even poisoned."

Those are nothing but a pack of blatant lies. Believe me, no politician in his right mind would dare face the fury of their constituents if they ever let our children suffer or go hungry.

In 1992, Clinton promised, among other things, to have the federal budget balanced and to "end the welfare program as we know it today." They are now out to kill the welfare reforms, using the base scare tactics as their weapon.

Which reminds me of Abe Lincoln's immortal remark: "You can fool all of the people some of the time; you can even fool some of the people all of the time; but you can't fool all of the people all of the time."

Less than two years hence, the electoral jury will deliver its harsh verdict upon the real villain.

"FLASH POINTS", ILLINOIS TIMES, MAY 11, 1995

BY RICK SHEREIKIS

I'm not what you'd call a fan of Rush Limbaugh's. But I do listen, as much as any normal person can be expected to, two or three minutes at a time at various points during his daily harangues against "big government" and "liberals." It used to be mostly out of curiosity, to hear what lines (and lies) Rush was feeding the ditto-heads, to use in place of their own ideas.

And, sometimes, over the noon hour, I channel surf, catching maybe half of Rush's TV show, where he acts up in front of folks who look like they've wandered in off a Christian Coalition tour bus. I'll watch a bit of that, to see what sort of sophomoric montage his editors have patched together each day, to put Rush's enemies in the least flattering light.

But since the Oklahoma City tragedy, it doesn't seem so amusing any more, the things Limbaugh plants in his followers' minds. His derisive comments about unflattering pictures of Donna Shalala or Chelsea Clinton don't seem so harmless now that we've grown more aware of all the blind hate for the federal government that's festering in the country, fed by the reckless talk that dominates our airwaves. Oklahoma City is a reminder that words have impact, and that people or groups that want to stir things up with broadcasts or publications need to be very careful about what they say, lest they drive an unstable mind into deadly action.

That's a message conservatives have been preaching for years, of course. They've been harsh on the television and movie industries, for example, suggesting that the mindless violence of certain productions (many of them, ironically, developed and promoted by right-wingers like Arnold Schwarzenegger and Rupert Murdoch) numbs people to the value of human life. And, these conservatives argue, the sexuality portrayed in much TV and movie programming is too provocative, inciting uncontrollable passions in impressionable young people.

But these conservative critics have done an interesting about-face in recent weeks, ever since President Clinton's generic complaint about the "many loud and angry voic-

to be continued

...es in America" who "spread hate" and "leave the impression..., by their very words, that violence is acceptable." These conservative voices, led by Limbaugh and convicted malefactors like Ollie North and G. Gordon Liddy, now say it's unfair to suggest that *their provocative words* have any impact on people. It's wrong, they say, to suggest that *their pugnacious rhetoric* might have anything to do with the militias, brotherhoods, and cults which have flourished and become bolder with the help of conservative talk radio.

An innocuous Murphy Brown episode will contaminate millions, they say; but their inflammatory political talk is Free Speech, bringing out opinions that are stifled by the "liberal" media.

But, as the President says, we shouldn't let these "purveyors of paranoia" get by with their attempt at a double standard.

Rush Lim-BOMB

And when he calls women who believe in equal rights "feminazis," and he makes fun of Donna Shalala's nose or Chelsea Clinton's hair, he's reducing the level of civility in public discourse. And when, as he did on the day of the Oklahoma City blast, he encourages callers to engage in reckless speculation about foreign terrorists who were in the country only because "our government has more rules about what's in our steak sauce than about who can come into the country," he's undermining people's respect for government while creating a hurtful climate in which Americans of "Middle Eastern appearance" are made to feel threatened.

Despite his malice and incendiary talk, however, Limbaugh looks downright cuddly compared to some of his fellow hosts. There's a guy named Chuck Baker, out of Colorado Springs, who has been heard to advocate the "elimination" of "traitors" in the Congress. There's New

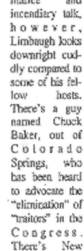

Limbaugh argues that he shouldn't be held responsible for the Oklahoma City blast, since he's never advocated the destruction of federal property. But when, speaking of attempts at environmental legislation, he says, "The second violent American revolution is just about—I've got my fingers just about a quarter inch apart—is just about that far away. Because these people are sick and tired of a bunch of bureaucrats in Washington driving into town and telling them what they can and can't do with their land"—when he talks like that, he can't pretend he might not set off a few loose cannons somewhere in a country full of newly energized John Birchers, Michigan Militia-men,

York City's Bob Grant (cordial host to willing guests like Al D'Amato, Rudolph Guiliani, and George Bush), who has called African Americans "sub-humanoids" and referred to former New York mayor David Dinkins, an African American, as "a washroom attendant." There's G. Gordon Liddy, running a clinic on the best ways to waste federal law enforcement officials.

There are even more extreme views, like Pat Robertson's anti-Semitic rantings about the New World Order, and the NRA's contemptuous talk about government, and the wacko things that go out on shortwave radio about how the Bible foretells all the trouble we're having now, thanks to the Tri-Lateral

to be continued

The use of religion by these extremists is especially dangerous, since it provides a spark of self-righteousness to the tinder of hostility in true believers. Put the notion that he's doing "God's work" in the mind of a Michigan Militia-man, say, and you've got a recipe for disaster. Pat Buchanan implies that he's doing God's patriotic will, as do Pat Robertson and Jerry Falwell and their legions of militant homophobics.

And, to bring the matter closer to home, so do the local members of STOPP, the anti-choice Springfield organization devoted to harassing Planned Parenthood and the local school administration. In their most recent newsletter, for example, they don't stop at mere disagreement with the pro-choice movement. "We are engaged in the Lord's work," they say, "...we have heard the Lord's wake-up call," which doesn't sound like a prelude to rational debate. But more disturbing yet, in the light of bombings and murders done in the name of the anti-choice movement, and in the more recent, glaring light of Oklahoma City, STOPP, armed with its conviction that they have direct-orders from some Higher Power, means to escalate its efforts: "We are going to get more aggressive," they announce in bold type. "We are going to get more aggressive and proactive as to what we say, as well as to whom it is going to be said."

So, at a time when talk radio has lowered the flash point for outbursts of violence and destruction, Rush Limbaugh and his conservative peers have raised the political temperature with their anti-government rhetoric; and Springfield's STOPP has vowed to get more aggressive and "proactive" in its campaign to deny Americans their Constitutional rights.

We can only hope the lessons of Oklahoma City will help them all pull back and remember the old saw about not crying "Fire!" in a crowded theater when there is no fire—especially if the theater is full of unstable people. And it would be nice if Rush would admit the power of his appeals to his listeners' basest instincts. When your fans call themselves "ditto-heads," you need to be extremely careful about what you say to them. ∎

SMOLDERING MCCARTHYISM

(Illinois Times, May 25, 1995)

Rick Shereikis' "Flash Points" smacks of bigotry and smoldering McCarthyism (see "Inklings," IT, May 11, 1995).

Being no fan of Rush Limbaugh's, Shereikis claims he still does listen to Rush's daily radio talk and even watches his TV show. How arrogant to refer to himself as a "normal person" and Rush's huge audience as "unstable and zombie-like."

While vigorously denouncing "reckless" talk-show hosts as irresponsible "purveyors of paranoia," Shereikis himself is resorting shamelessly to the very extremist tactics he deplores. He tears into Rush Limbaugh—Vice President Al Gore not too long ago praised him as one of the most distinguished Americans—portraying him as the darkest force of violence by the name of "Rush LimBOMB." The desperate attempt to blame the Oklahoma tragedy on Rush and his fellow conservative talk show hosts is just ludicrous. Indeed, it is tilting at windmills. He would be well advised to recollect for a while that some idiot crashed the plane into the White House compound, and that just last October, the White House was again fired upon by another jerk in broad daylight.

Also, it is worthwhile to note here that psychotic patients, schizophrenic or paranoid, are greatly influenced by internal stimuli rather than outside forces. This makes mental cases so difficult to treat.

Violence has no place in a democratic society like ours, and is absolutely unacceptable. What happened at Waco, Texas, in no way justifies the bombing of the Oklahoma City federal building last month. However, "revolution" takes place at voting booths. Haven't we all witnessed last year the Democrats lose their forty years control of Congress?

Loony perpetrators of the most heinous crimes should be prosecuted as such, and they must not be victimized in any way, shape or form.

Personal Rebuttal:
by Rick Shereikis, May 26, 1995

May 26

Dear Dr. Kim:

While you, of course, have every right to disagree with my views on Rush Limbaugh and his peers, you also have a responsibility to represent what I said with some degree of accuracy and to respond to what I actually said, rather than to what you imagined.

You will look in vain in my column for a reference to anyone as "zombie-like," for example, although by putting that phrase in quotation marks, you implied that I had used it. If you had read carefully, you might also have noticed that I didn't say that Limbaugh's regular audience was "unstable," but that this country is full of unstable people who might possibly be ignited by inflammatory talk. The enclosed New York _Times_ pieces ("Home on the Range" and "Paramilitary Group Leaders. . .") make that pretty clear; and it seems plausible to suggest that the Limbaughs, Liddys, and Norths, not to mention the Robertsons and Falwells, have helped legitimize bigotry, homophobia, and paranoid fear of the government in the same ways in which Ronald Reagan legitimized racism and greed during his time in office.

As for the "Lim-BOMB" reference, that was not part of the copy I turned in. Editors pick the art work and the captions, and quite frankly I hadn't even noticed the "Lim-BOMB" caption until your letter made me look for it. Given an option, I wouldn't have used that cartoon or that caption.

Also, I'm not sure it's fair to characterize my column as an example of "extremist tactics." I didn't say that Limbaugh, et. al., had <u>caused</u> the Oklahoma City bombing. I did say that people who reach vast audiences had better be careful about what they say, because there are loose cannons out there, and you never know what's going to set them off (see the NY _Times_ pieces). I would suggest that Liddy's talk about how to kill government agents speaks for itself as real "extremism," as do the rantings of STOPP, which I also cited, and which I can't believe you'd condone.

Finally, what's "extreme" depends on your perspective, I guess. I called Liddy and Oliver North "convicted malefactors" because that's what they are, literally. I called Limbaugh's fans "ditto-heads" because that's what they call themselves, apparently with pride. I called Pat Robertson an "anti-Semite" because his writings make that clear (as a recent <u>New York Review of Books</u> article revealed); and I called Robertson and Jerry Falwell "militant homophobics" because their public statements make clear that the sympathies of these "Christian" leaders don't extend to homosexuals.

I appreciate your taking the time to write. But you should be more careful with your use of quotation marks and, to be fair, more careful not to misrepresent the views of others.

Sincerely,

Rick Shereikis

P.S. Thought you might also find the enclosed column on the N.R.A. interesting. Wouldn't it be nice if more conservative leaders would join George Bush in separating themselves from strident, inflammatory rhetoric of the sort in which that extremist organization engages?

WHY MUST WE ALWAYS
SEEK A FALL GUY

(The State Journal-Register, June 5, 1995)

In the wake of the Okalahoma City federal building blast, there seems to be a somewhat unsettling trend emerging from Washington. Their modus operandi is first seek out a fall guy to blame rather than take the responsibility for the disaster.

While the nation was literally reeling from the sheer enormity of the Oklahoma tragedy, the president took the bully pulpit to lambaste radio talk show hosts as "spreaders of anger and hatred" and "purveyors of paranoia."

Rhetoric is one thing, but politicizing the tragic event is another. Obviously, this preposterous ad hominem charge didn't stick at all. As a matter of fact, it seems to have backfired.

Now, they change the tune to target the national Rifle Association as if it were the hotbed of crimes. Granted, the NRA leadership committed an inane mistake by referring to federal law enforcement agents as "jack-booted thugs." Some of the members followed suit when former President George Bush resigned his lifetime membership in protest against the ridiculous accusations. It seems that the NRA has already paid a hefty price for their boo-boo.

Now enters the unheard-of, mind-boggling "tank-jacking" incident that recently unfolded dramatically in San Diego. After all, who could be held accountable for this loony rampage? The National Guard, NRA or tank manufacturers?

PRAISES FOR PILOT
OUT OF PROPORTION

(The State Journal-Register, June 22, 1995)

How much relieved and happy we were to see Capt. Scott O'Grady return home safe from his hellish ordeal in the former Yugoslavia.

But superfluous praises heaped upon him as "a hero" during the welcome ceremony from Andrew Air Force Base to the White House seemed to be embarrassingly out of proportion with the picture-perfect performance of his mission.

This is not intended at all to take away from the brave captain's remarkable feat. Far from it. Surely, Capt. O'Grady should be looked upon as a role model for all aspiring Air Force pilots.

The thing that strikes us most about the "heroic" young pilot is his self-effacing humbleness: On numerous occasions he thanked God profusely for his life and never failed to pay tribute to the U.S. crack rescue team for his survival.

Perhaps Capt. O'Grady is being degraded by lionizing him as "a hero."

PUZZLED BY ATTITUDE
OF WWII REVISIONISTS

(The State Journal-Register, August 29, 1995)

The 50th anniversary of the end of World War II has seen both armchair strategists and history revisionists come out of the woodwork.

Call V-J Day by any other name and wouldn't it still be our triumphant victory over Japan which forced us into the Pacific War with their sneaky Pearl Harbor attack?

How inscrutable it is, indeed, that some Americans now appear to be increasingly more guilt-laden with our first use of the atomic bombs than the Japanese! Perhaps the picture of the deadly blast with mushroom clouds is carved in the minds of all people, whereas the graphic counterpart of Japan's appalling brutality and atrocities during the war is entirely missing.

Half a century later, the Japanese are still visibly struggling to deal with their past wrongs, as evidenced by their prime minister's mealy-mouthed apology to the rest of the world on the commemorative occasion.

Be that as it may, history should be judged in the context of times. The ailment of might-have-been syndrome currently prevalent among babyboomers stems largely from their naïve idealism coupled with idle second-guessing.

IDLE SECOND GUESSING

(Illinois Times, September 7, 1995)

The fiftieth anniversary of the end of World War II has seen both armchair strategists and history revisionists come out of the woodwork.

Call V-J Day by any other name and wouldn't it still be our triumphant victory over Japan which forced us into the Pacific War with their sneaky Pearl Harbor attack?

How inscrutable it is, indeed, that some Americans now appear to be increasingly more guilt-ladened with our first use of the atomic bombs than the Japanese! Perhaps the picture of the deadly blast with mushroom clouds is carved in the minds of all people, whereas the graphic counterpart of Japan's appalling brutality and atrocities during the war is entirely missing.

Half a century later, the Japanese are still visibly struggling to deal with their past wrongs, as evidenced by their prime minister's mealy-mouthed apology to the rest of the world on the commemorative occasion.

Be that as it may, history should be judged in the context of times. The ailment of might-have-been syndrome currently prevalent among baby boomers stems largely from their naïve idealism coupled with idle second-guessing.

ENGLISH NEEDS TO BE
OUR OFFICIAL LANGUAGE

(The State Journal-Register, September 17, 1995)

Debate heats up again as to whether English finally should be made our official language. This very issue can be compelling yet divisive, particularly at a time when the recent demography of the United States shows 8.7 percent of its population to be foreign born.

Being the land of immigrants from every corner of the Earth, our country certainly deserves the sobriquet of "ethnic kaleidoscope." Yet, unless we have one common language with which to communicate as the unifying means and bonds of multi-ethnic communities, our great society will ultimately end up being a Tower of Babel.

The designation of English as our official language will, in no way, denigrate or belittle our rich and vibrant cultural diversity.

We have one national anthem to sing together, Old Glory as our flag for which to rally, soaring bald eagle as our national symbol as well as the sweet-smelling rose as our national flower. How odd it is, then, that we still lack one official language—English—as our national language.

It is about time that Congress passed the bill to declare English the official language of the United States of America.

ENGLISH SHOULD NOT BE OFFICIAL LANGUAGE

(The State Journal-Register, September 24, 1995)

To the Editor,

I read the letter Dr. Chansoo Kim wrote in the September 17 edition with amazement. I cannot believe we are still debating this innocuous issue in this country.

Over 200 years of history and no official language. Decades of opening the doors to the Irish, Italians, Germans and other groups that slowly but surely integrated to the "main" culture-language and all.

It should be noted that for decades government agencies including the courts, have provided for interpretation for those who do not speak or understand English.

America has always strived for the principles of inclusion and this method has proven to keep and promote a vibrant culture. Last July 18 Reps. Jose E. Serrano and Ileana Ros-Lehtinen introduced an English-plus resolution in Congress. The resolution promotes the learning and usage of the many languages spoken in the United States. Serrano said: "English-plus affirms our Democratic principles of freedom of expression and respect for different opinions, cultures and religions.

This country has proven to be the greatest power in human history. Its unique blend of peoples and the principles and freedoms we know cannot and should not be subjugated to the notion that without an official language we will succumb. Do you know of any nation with an official language that is greater than America? I don't think so.

Hector L. Torregrosa
Springfield

'POLITICALLY CORRECT' BIBLE IS TOO MUCH

(The State Journal-Register, December 3, 1995)

We find ourselves caught up in the surging tide of political correctness movement which we may call the juggernaut of the century. Virtually, nothing will remain unscathed from the assault, and its impact is so penetrating that it is felt everywhere in our society.

As a case in point, we can cite, among other things, the forthcoming "inclusive" version of the New Testament and Psalms which purports to be gender-neutral, getting rid of what they call insensitive and discriminatory words in the Bible, namely light, dark, the right hand, etc.

According to Isaiah 40:8, "the grass withers and the flowers fall but the word of the Lord stands forever." What's more, 2 Timothy 3:16-17 also tells us, "All scripture is inspired by God and profitable for teaching, for reproof, for correction, and for training in righteousness, that the man of God may be complete, equipped for every good work."

Could Almighty God ever be defaulted for creating man and woman? How dare we tamper with the Holy Book!

The upcoming "political-correct" version of the Bible is finally pushing us over the cliff.

'STARVE-MOUTHING'

(Chicago Tribune, January 30, 1996)

Regarding your Jan. 2 editorial titled "Danger on the Korean peninsula".

With their moribund economy on its death bed, North Koreans are widely reported to face the specter of mass starvation this winter; more than 2 million poor children will either die or suffer from severe malnutrition.

Such being the plight, Pyongyang no longer shies away from begging on a grand scale for food worldwide. The officials are blaming the current crisis of a critical food shortage on the vagaries of Mother Nature—"a double whammy of the worst floods and famine," which they did suffer last year. But in reality, the devastating natural disasters are the straw that broke the camel's back.

Ironically, what's equally unsettling and even somewhat enigmatic is the news that North Korean troops are being mobilized en masse for deployment along the demilitarized zone. How could they possibly go hungry and still pursue their hostile operations against the South? Are they just "starve-mouthing" to prop up the crumbling economy?

It is imperative, therefore, that the Western world community's humanitarian relief effort go directly to a starving population in North Korea. Also, further future economic assistance, if any, should be tied to the drastic reform of their economic system.

DANGEROUS TENSIONS BETWEEN CHINA, TAIWAN

(The State Journal-Register, March 6, 1996)

While a large number of U.S. troops are being committed to the fragile Bosnian peace-keeping mission, another huge killer storm is brewing off the Strait of Taiwan; tensions are dangerously escalating to a flashpoint between China and its runaway province, Taiwan.

As we are headed into the November presidential election, what better time for our adversaries to take advantage of the murky domestic political climate in which the rancorous divisiveness and the growing mistrust of government prevail among its voters?

By all indications, it seems that China is hell-bent in the name of "reunification" to recapture Taiwan by force.

The Beijing regime knows full well—as we do—that short of direct military confrontation, we won't be able to take any other forceful measures against their potential invasion of Taiwan, an economic powerhouse in Asia.

Predictably, Washington's recent official response to China's belligerent moves—"It takes two to tango. It takes two to engage," etc.—sounds awfully hollow. To make matters worse, what if renegade North Korea jumps on the "reunification bandwagon" with its daredevil and last gasp attack into Seoul?

Clearly, as the regional crisis for security deepens, strong U.S. global leadership is called for now more than ever before.

This time around, unlike 1992, could it be "It's foreign policy, stupid?"

DANGEROUS TENSIONS BETWEEN CHINA, TAIWAN

3/6/96

Dear Sir,

To merely let you know how I enjoy your letters to the local Editor of our newspaper.

They are so informative, particularly your letter of today on the subject of China/Taiwan. We dumb Americans, you know, need to know more. Keep your letters coming!

Roy Bertelli
Springfield

FBI WILLINGLY COMPLIED WITH REQUEST FOR FILES

(The State Journal-Register, June 30, 1996)

The White House files scandal causes the American public a grave concern about the Federal Privacy Act. They are also deeply troubled to hear the FBI director openly announce, "The FBI and I were victimized by the White House when it obtained the confidential files."

Which brings us to raise a fundamental question. Who are really the victims of this Watergate-style dirty trick? Of course, they are none other than over 400 prominent Americans whose personal background files have been snooped into for some arcane reasons. What's more, how could one overlook the unsettling fact that the FBI finds itself in the center of the storm?

As the old adage goes, it takes two to tango—the White House requested the files and the FBI willingly complied with the request.

We just wish the new White House scandal were simply "a completely honest bureaucratic snafu." But when the FBI director recently slammed the charges against the White House with egregious violations of privacy, the whole situation now turns far more serious and intriguingly complex than they let on.

As the "blunder" saga slowly unfolds, we believe that the truth will speak for itself.

PAR FOR THE COURSE

(Chicago Tribune, September 24, 1996)

Nothing could be more puzzling to us than the Chicago Tribune's front page headline "Sub Mystery Puzzles Korea." It sounds as if Pyongyang had given up its one and only grandiose agenda which is reunification of the Korean Peninsula on its own terms. Are we, indeed, naïve enough to believe that the leopard can change its spots?

After all, for the past 46 years the North Korean regime has been relentlessly engaging in all kinds of reprehensible terror acts against the South. The latest "beached" spy submarine incidence is par for the course and shouldn't come as a surprise to Seoul.

According to the September 1st issue of Parade, Kim Jong II, a tinhorn dictator splurged $134 million on redecorating his residence while his poor people are facing stark famine due to the recurrent ravaging floods. So far, the U.S. reportedly has given $8.4 million in aid through the U.N. program.

Certainly, we do want assurances that the donated food goes to North Korea's 23 million starving people, not to its repressive Army and daredevil suicidal commandoes.

CARPAL TUNNEL ET AL

(Illinois Times, December 5-11, 1996)

This response is intended to keep readers up to speed on the current concept of cumulative trauma disorders (CTDs) in the workplace [see "Consumers Carp About Carpal Tunnel," IT, November 21, 1996].

According to the U.S. Bureau of Labor Statistics, the incidence of CTDs has increased dramatically in recent years. Since 1989, these injuries have accounted for more than 50 percent of all occupational illnesses reported in the U.S. Every year, some 200,000 Americans are reported to develop CTDs from repetitive use of their hands at work.

Cumulative trauma disorders, no longer a mystery, are now dubbed as "the occupational disorder of the 1990s." Under the general rubric of CTDs fall various medical conditions such as tenosynovitis, wrist and shoulder tendonitis, De-Quervain's tenosynovitis, epicondylitis, carpal tunnel syndrome, and ulnar nerve entrapment, etc.

Carpal tunnel Syndrome (CTS) is by far the most common and disabling cumulative trauma disorder. Nowadays CTS is bandied about among both blue and white collar workers. However, the whole issue of CTDs or RSIs (repetitive strain injuries) appears to be far more complex.

A host of certain underlying medical conditions predispose us to carpal tunnel syndrome. They are, among other things, Colles' fracture, rheumatoid arthritis, diabetes, hypothyroidism, (myxedema), pregnancy, morbid obesity, amyloidosis, collagen vascular disease, degenerative arthritis and ganglion cysts, etc. It is a matter of common medical knowledge that CTS occurs predominantly among women between the ages of twenty-five and sixty, the ratio being about four to one.

Medical considerations aside, we have seen CTS develop from many common hobbies: bicycling, gardening, cooking, sewing, sanding, drilling, painting, knitting, crocheting, and even playing musical instruments. We can see that avocational or recreational activities outside of the job are just as important as the vocational factors.

According to a June 1992 Mayo Clinic report, one of the most frequently listed occupations of patients with CTS in Rochester, Minnesota (1961 through 1980) is homemaker, followed by retired person. Surprisingly, female gender with use of oral contraceptive is reported to be the strongest of risk factors. Furthermore, several reports have described an association between CTS and bilateral oophorectomy (removal of the ovaries). The high incidence of CTS in perimenopausal women also suggests the changes in ovarian function or use of exogenous estrogens may be important in the development of CTS. To make matters worse, hereditary cases of CTS are being increasingly reported.

Thus, the complexity of CTS dictates a more thorough assessment of each work-related CTS case from the medical, vocational, avocational and genetic viewpoints. Otherwise, ergonomics and workplace modifications may only play a limited role as a preventative measure.

After all, occupational CTS is only one of several major risk factors.

BEARDSTOWN LADIES PUT TOWN ON GLOBAL MAP

(The State Journal-Register, February 6, 1997)

Back in 1984, Beardstown attracted national media attention when the Occupational Safety and Health Administration (OSHA) slapped its first citation on the then Oscar Mayer pork processing plant for "an endemic" outbreak of carpal tunnel syndrome among its workers.

It could be said from the medical perspective that the current hot potato issue of Repetitive Strain Injuries or Cumulative Trauma Disorders took its origin from Beardstown.

Now thanks to the Beardstown Ladies Investment club, Beardstown has drastically changed its image from CTS breeding grounds to a Mecca for private investors clubs.

Beardstown Ladies, much to the envy of Wall Street pundits, have instantly become much sought after international celebrities by virtue of their uncanny investing skills and other prolific publications—one best seller after another in as many years.

True to form, the ladies just don't rest on their own laurels. They are again out to spread financial gospel with their third book, "Smart Spending for Big Savings."

It is no stretch at all to say we can't think of any better role model for American women, young and old alike, than the Beardstown Ladies.

Kudos to the proverbial Beardstown Ladies for putting their hometown on the global map.

ASIAN-BASHING

(Chicago Tribune, March 3, 1997)

Some of the mainstream print media have been doing a yeoman's job in tracking down the Asian fund-raising connections intricately interwoven with the White House and the Democratic National Committee.

Recently, veteran investigative reporter Bob Woodward of the Washington Post, citing reliable intelligence intercepts weighed in with his earth-shaking revelation of the Chinese Embassy involvement in steering money to the presidential campaign.

Even President Clinton expressed his outright dismay and anger in his press conference over the news of Chinese contributions to "one of the political parties."

Ironically, at a time when all those almost daily leaks finally turned into a flood, an ex-congressman of California, a would-be chief guardian of Asian-American rights, calls for a formation of an anti-defamation league, allegedly out of fears that "all law-abiding Asian citizens and legal immigrants would be lumped together and victimized by what's going on with the Asian-bashing as a result of these fund-raising investigations.

He even went so far as to dredge up the horrible memories of the Japanese internment camp during World War II. Could this be simply a figment of the imagination or a case of paranoia?

The fact is, a few Asian-American hustlers or secret Asian agents give the entire community a black-eye, for they have shamelessly taken advantage of their unscrupulous fellow-Asians as point men while ferociously working for their own hidden agendas.

This burgeoning political scandal of foreign campaign contributions should in no way be deflected or trivialized as an "Asian-bashing." As the President aptly stated, "we need to get to the bottom of it." If we ever needed an independent counsel investigation, this is the time for it—for the sake of our national security.

GLAD GENDER NEUTRAL
BIBLE IDEA PUT ON ICE

(The State Journal-Register, June 26, 1997)

Not long ago, the International Bible Society triggered a barrage of protests from the Christian community with its politically correct proposal for a gender-neutral version of the Bible.

However, we now welcome the society's apparent change of heart under intense pressure; the controversial inclusive edition of the NIV is finally put on ice.

Standing on the threshold of human cloning, perhaps we all suffer from the abominable delusion of omnipotence. From Genesis 11, we see our ancestors trying to build a city with a tower that reaches the sky, so that they could make a name for themselves. But God didn't like the idea and destroyed the tower. The reason God offered for the tower of Babel is, "this is just the beginning of what they are going to do. Soon, they will be able to do anything they want."

The Apostle John, in Revelation (22:18-19), the last book of the Bible, issues a stern warning to us, "If anyone adds anything to what's written here, God will add to that person the plagues described in this book. And if anyone removes any of the words of this prophetic book, God will remove that person's share in the tree of life."

Nations rise and fall. But the word of God will stand forever.

BOXING REVEALS SADISTIC ASPECT OF HUMAN NATURE

(The State Journal-Register, July 15, 1997)

The most gruesome incidence of a world-class boxer taking a bite out of his opponent's ear in the recent bout will likely reignite debate on an outright ban of boxing as a sporting event.

As we are aware, in some parts of the world people enjoy just as much a bull-fight, cock-fight, or dog-fight as a popular entertainment. But "man-fight" as boxing, for one thing, clearly reveals the hidden sadistic aspect of human nature, if not animalistic.

First blows exchanged as in pummeling or pounding invariably cause boxers serious brain damage over time. One of the early signs of the brain damaged is unpredictable emotional outbursts or acting in such a way that they snap at the slightest provocation.

Pugilistic dementia (boxer's dementia) is one good example of permanent brain damage while punch drunkness with a haymaker may result from a mild degree of cerebral insult.

Some years back, the American Medical Association took its stand against boxing solely for medical reasons. It's about time we paid heed to the AMA's strong disapproval of the boxing game.

VIAGRA HAS OPENED
FLOODGATE ON ISSUES

(The State Journal-Register, May 27, 1998)

Barely three months on the market, Pfizer's Viagra has already become a blockbuster. It could very well be the drug of the year, if not the century.

The current Viagra craze, despite its hefty price, is readily understood since 30 million American males experience some type of erectile dysfunction, and the new drug is proven quite efficacious in well over 80 percent of patients with minimal side effects.

Yet, Viagra now seems to have opened a floodgate on social and ethical issues, setting the stage for serious debate on the fundamental issue of who pays for what—lifestyle vs. treatment.

In the majority of cases, Viagra is viewed mainly as lifestyle-enhancing with improved performance, although it can be prescribed as a form of treatment in some intractable cases of impotence.

The $64 question, is should health insurances pay for lifestyle-enhancing drugs such as Viagra? If so, how many pills per month? Any age limits, etc?

No sooner did some health insurance carriers announce willingness to reimburse their claimants for Viagra than woman activist demanded that insurers also pay for contraceptive pills. They strongly argue that contraception is to females what Viagra is to males.

Last but not least, as with any new "wonder" drug, potential wild abuses of Viagra are also feared among younger people.

LOWER MORAL STANDARDS ARE THE MAJOR CULPRIT

(The State Journal-Register, June 19, 1998)

While the whole Asian region is in the midst of its worst financial crisis, teetering on the verge of collapse, we Americans are literally in the nirvana of Goldilocks economy with low inflation rates and steady growth.

As icing on the cake, the Clinton administration projects a budget surplus this year to the tune of $40 billion for the first time since the Nixon era.

But something hither-to-unheard of and altogether frightening is seriously threatening our children at this time of unprecedented prosperity. The bogeyman is the recent rash of school shooting rampages by one teen after another that have swept the country from West Paducah, Ky., to Jonesboro, Ark., to Springfield, Ore.

What turns schoolyards into a killing field? Obviously, it is not the economy. Then, could it really be a symptom of changing culture?

Rather than frantically look for easy targets or usual scapegoats on which to blame this senseless carnage, such as teen smoking, TV violence, gun control, etc., we may have to confront the ghastly issue head-on and honestly admit that we have nothing else to blame but ourselves.

To the extent that the "nothing-is-wrong" mentality or "victimization syndrome" permeates our present-day society, we have unscrupulously lowered our moral standards, let alone dumbed down our educational standards.

We may be able to legislate smoking bans or strict gun control, but we can't legislate morality.

Reader Correspondence

CITIZENS FOR TRADITIONAL VALUES
- OF CENTRAL ILLINOIS -

P.O. BOX 9744
SPRINGFIELD, IL 62791-9744

July 9, 1998

Chansoo Kim, M.D.
39 Glen Eagle Drive
Springfield, IL 62704

Dear Dr. Kim:

I read your recent letter to the editor in the *State Journal Register* and appreciated your thoughts. I am very thankful that there are individuals such as yourself willing to take the time and effort to voice concerns about the moral decay in our community/nation.

Since we share some of the same viewpoints, I thought you might enjoy seeing Citizens for Traditional Values' newsletter. Citizens for Traditional Values is an organization formed in 1997 by individuals in Sangamon County.

Sincerely,

Chris Blankenship
Administrative Assistant CTV

787-7343

ONLY IN AMERICA

(Chicago Tribune, June 30, 1998)

A June 9 Page 1 story ("More school daycare set for students' kids") hit us with a jolting reminder that LBJ's Great Society finally has come to fruition; now the Chicago Public Schools system even provides in-house daycare centers for teenage mothers lest they should drop out of school and fall into the chronic poverty associated with teen motherhood.

The Clinton administration leans on Medicaid programs to pick up the tab for Viagra, a popular impotence drug.

Only in America: There are free condoms for teenagers, free day care for teen moms, free needles for drug addicts and free Viagra for some needy people who wish to enrich their sex life.

America, what a country!

WHAT WILL THE FATE OF GOV. CHILES BE?

(The State Journal-Register, July 26, 1998)

These days the Sunshine State is anything but sunshine. It's more like an inferno.

Their worst wildfires in history have been blazing away since the Memorial Day weekend, exacting a heavy toll on property. It's now estimated that half a million acres have been scorched, leaving several hundred people homeless.

Worse yet, a prolonged spell of drought has made it even more difficult to prevent the fires from spreading.

Apparently, out of desperation, Lawton Chiles, governor of Florida, began to pray to God for much-needed rain and reportedly also entreated his fellow Floridians to join him in prayer.

Which reminds us vividly of a ludicrous and shameful incident in the Bronx, New York City, where a school teacher recently was summarily dismissed for no other reason than mentioning "god" and "heaven" in her classroom. The First amendment (separation of church and state), they say, is at stake.

We wonder loudly what will befall Gov. Chiles and his political career.

ROEPER TAKEN TO TASK
FOR COLUMN ON MONICA

(The State Journal-Register, September 2, 1998)

Richard Roeper's Aug. 9 column reminds us of what yellow journalism is all about.

Back in early January, when Vernon Jordan, the most astute and influential corporate lawyer in Washington, D.C., the beltway vouched for Monica Lewinsky as a "vibrant and promising young lady," Mr. Roeper should have in no time leaped out, and as he wished he should have "stood on a mountaintop and screamed at the top of his lungs"; Not! "Monica is a 'babbling bar room floozy.'"

Mr. Roeper, why now, seven months later? Granted, Monica received transactional immunity from the independent counsel and she has already testified before the grand jury against the president. Ironically, Mr. Roeper also portrays Monica as a sexual predator with the blue dress on and the President as her helpless victim.

If we jog our memory, Paula Jones also had been trashed as a trailer park floozy when she filed a suit against the President for sexual harassment.

Just as trailer park residents are unfairly smeared and stigmatized, so are now young ladies with the blue dress on.

Nevertheless, to paraphrase the feisty 33rd President Harry S. Truman, no matter how it ends, the buck stops with the President, not with Monica.

TREATMENT OF ADMIRAL SHOWS A DOUBLE STANDARD

(The State Journal-Register, December 15, 1998)

The very latest news that "a U.S. Navy Admiral retires over adultery charges" literally knocks our socks off.

According to one Gallup poll after another conducted over the years, the majority of Americans reportedly hold the belief that sex and perjury is no big deal. Adultery, we are being admonished, is none of our business, as it is consensual sex between two adults. Rather, we should leave the matter entirely up to the person involved and his spouse and family.

Beats me, then, how Rear Admiral John T. Scudi was forced to retire at a lower rank with a reduced pension. To add insult to injury, Scudi will be placed under 30-day arrest in his quarters and will eventually receive a punitive letter of reprimand for his actions.

This makes us wonder whether we are living in two different worlds. What do we make out of this anachronistic, unfair treatment? Is this the Orwellian double-think or simply a double standard?

While Congress is making every conceivable effort to lower the bar, it is indeed too bad that the Admiral could not beat the rap.

WOULD YOU SAY YOU "HAD SEX" IF . . . ?

(JAMA, January 20, 1999—Vol. 281, No. 3)

Stephanie A. Sanders, PhD
June Machover Reinisch, PhD

Author Affiliations: The Kinsey Institute for Research in Sex, Gender, and Reproduction (Drs Sanders and Reinisch) and Gender Studies (Dr Sanders) Indiana University, and R² Science Communications Inc (Dr Reinisch), Bloomington; and the Institute of Preventative Medicine, Copenhagen University Hospital, Copenhagen, Denmark (Dr Reinisch).

Context The current public debate regarding whether oral sex constitutes having "had sex" or sexual relations has reflected a lack of empirical data on how Americans as a population define these terms.

Objective To determine which interactions individuals would consider as having "had sex."

Methods A question was included in a survey conducted in 1991 that explored sexual behaviors and attitudes among a random stratified sample of 599 students representative of the undergraduate population of a state university in the Midwest.

Participants The participants originated from 29 states, including all 4 US Census Bureau geographic regions. Approximately 79% classified themselves as politically moderate to conservative.

Chansoo Kim, M.D.

Main Outcome Measure Percentage of respondents who believed the interaction described constituted having "had sex."

Results Individual attitudes varied regarding behaviors defined as having "had sex": 59% (95% confidence interval, 54%—63%) of respondents indicated that oral-genital contact did not constitute having "had sex" with a partner. Nineteen percent responded similarly regarding penile-anal intercourse.

Conclusions The findings support the view that Americans hold widely divergent opinions about what behaviors do, and do not constitute having "had sex."

Please note that the above is the original abstract of the most controversial research paper ever published in the JAMA (Journal of American Medical Association).

MOTIVES OF SEX ARTICLE
NOT HARD TO FATHOM

(The State Journal-Register, February 14, 1999)

Hard at heels of the Sunbeam debacle, AMA again finds itself in hot water, this time over the abrupt firing of its journal editor.

Dr. George Lundberg apparently got the ax for allowing a "politically motivated" sex research article to be published in the Jan. 20, 1999, issue of JAMA.

In a nutshell, the survey conducted in 1991 took a random sample of 599 undergraduate students in the Midwest. Approximately 79 percent of the study group classified themselves as politically moderate to conservative. What's intriguingly interesting, there were more registered Republicans (342 percent) than Democrats (19 percent) while 7 percent identified themselves as Independents.

According to the survey results, the majority of the respondents (59 percent) indicated the oral genital contact did not constitute having "had sex" with a partner.

What timely revelation to U.S. Senators at the height of the impeachment trial!

In order to fathom the ulterior motives behind the controversial sex survey, one only has to read the problematic article. It sure doesn't take an M.D. degree to do so.

P.S.: President William Jefferson Clinton was impeached by the House on Saturday (12/19/98) for perjury and obstruction of justice.

The 42nd Chief Executive thus became the second since the nation's founding to be ordered to stand trial in the Senate.

IT TAKES A GOOD, SOLID FAMILY TO RAISE A CHILD

(The State Journal-Register, September 23, 1999)

Perhaps The State Journal-Register's recent story about Nathan Kester of New Berlin may shed some light on the unnerving social issue of escalating school violence.

Nathan, born with severe hearing impairment and abandoned by his birth parents in Korea, was fortunately adopted at age 3 by a warm-hearted, deaf couple in New Berlin.

Nothing could stop him from diligently pursuing his education and finally earning him the Very Best in Youth award sponsored by Nestle. Nathan also graduated from the Illinois School for the Deaf as a valedictorian. Known as a voracious reader, he now aspires to become a medical doctor. It seems as if the sky were the limit for him.

According to a "scarred psychology" theory which lately popped up out of nowhere, Nathan was destined to be a basket case; not only wouldn't he amount to much, but he would be a potential perpetrator of some crime. But the only thing that clearly sets Nathan apart from other troubled kids is his secure foundation of family support and love.

We are often told that it takes a village to raise a child. After all, it also may take a good, solid family to raise a child. It's time we put family values on the front burner.

WILL'S COLUMN ABOUT NAVY OFFICER WAS INSPIRING

(The State Journal-Register, November 24, 1999)

It is altogether uplifting and reassuring to read George Will's column about a young Navy officer.

Here is a graduate of the Navy ROTC at the University of North Carolina who on New Year's Eve 1998 took his first tour of duty aboard the USS Blue Ridge. Only eight months later, it so happened that one of the sailors on the deck was involved in a freaky yet mortal accident. Ensign Daniel Johnson immediately endangered himself in order to rescue the sailor who came within an eyelash of losing his life.

Thanks to the young officer's valiant feats, the sailor's life was saved but the ensign himself ends up being a double below-knee amputee at the tender age of 23.

What a tragic setback such a promising young man has suffered early on in his life! Yet, he just takes it in stride, saying that "there is more of him leaving the Navy than entered it."

There is no recondite lesson to be learned from this episode. Indeed, Ensign Johnson can be hailed as the epitome of honor and responsibility. Let us pray for this brave young man's speedy rehabilitation and heavenly rewards in his new endeavor.

AN OUNCE OF PREVENTION
WORTH A POUND OF CURE

(The State Journal-Register, September 9, 2000)

Sudden infant death syndrome (SIDS), or what used to be called crib death, is the sudden, unexplained death of a baby under a year.

It was kind of a medical mystery for decades until researchers recently noted a close link between the deaths and babies who slept on their stomachs. Research also has proven that keeping a baby on its back reduces the risk of SIDS by 40 to 50 percent.

Thus, the nationwide "Back to Sleep" campaign was vigorously launched jointly in 1994 by the American Academy of Pediatrics and the U.S. government.

As a result, more parents place their babies to sleep on the back. Now, the byproduct of the "Back to Sleep" campaign is the baby's positional plagiocephaly. Though a mouthful medical term, it is simply the misshapen head or flat-headed. Nowadays, it seems that many parents are unduly alarmed by the prospect of having their flat-headed babies from sleeping on their back.

Fortunately, since a newborn baby's skull is soft and malleable, the baby's head can be practically molded in a symmetric manner only if the parents take their vigilant efforts to change the baby's head position from back to sides at regular intervals.

As the old adage goes, "An ounce of prevention is worth a pound of cure."

DON'T PLAY INTO THE HANDS OF NORTH KOREAN DICTATOR

(The State Journal-Register, December 10, 2000)

Secretary of State Albright's recent visit to North Korea was whooped up by the media as a diplomatic masterstroke to help close the final chapter of the Cold War. However, such a ballyhoo over quickening U.S.—North Korea diplomatic maneuvers calls for some personal observations.

For openers, Kim Jong II of North Korea, once mocked as a tinhorn dictator in a small, reclusive, yet starving, communist country, is suddenly catapulted as sort of a respectable world leader. As we are well aware, South Korean President Kim Dae Jung made a history-making visit to Pyongyang in June for the summit meeting with a paramount leader in the North. This bold move helped President Kim to win a Nobel Peace prize for the year 2000. Kim Jong II has yet to make his a return visit.

Surely we have a long way to go before we ever see permanent peace on the Korean Peninsula with its ultimate reunification. But two Koreas, as principal players, have got to continue their ongoing dialogues without interruption.

Already some South Korean officials voice their concern that "the speed at which Pyongyang-Washington relations are moving is slowing progress between two Koreas." Which raises a serious question: Is Washington trying to steal the show from Seoul? Or are we simply playing in the hands of the Great Leader Kim?

RHETORIC, HYPERBOLE DON'T HAVE IMPACT ON ECONOMY

(The State Journal-Register, January 31, 2001)

These days bad news about U.S. economy seems to be coming out of the woodwork. In the midst of the current market downturn with a rash of sell-offs, somebody is accused of "talking the economy down just to push his political agenda."

Could the president or Fed chairman ever talk the economy down into recession? The answer may require a brief look at the past history. Back in 1928 when Herbert C. Hoover ran for president, his campaign slogan was "a chicken in every pot." Indeed he did try to talk the economy up, firmly believing that recovery was just around the corner. Yet, President Hoover ended up having presided over the Great Depression of 1929.

As lately as 1996, Alan Greenspan, the mighty Fed chairman, openly mused about that memorable, catchy phrase "irrational exuberance," obviously in a deliberate effort to browbeat a Goldilocks economy into "rational behavior." A stern warning shot from the most powerful central banker notwithstanding, the stock market just shrugged it off and got instead revved up, roaring along to reach one record high after another.

Now, with telltale signs of significant slowing down virtually in every sector of economy, the nation's longest bull market is surely running out of steam. Soft landing of recession hinges on hard economic data, not rhetoric or hyperbole.

JAPANESE CAR COMPANY BENEFITED MOST FROM STUNT

(The State Journal-Register, March 12, 2001)

As promised, President Bush sent his 10-year, $1.6 trillion tax cut plan to Congress. Just as expected, Democrats on the Hill immediately began to mount their vigorous campaign against it, howling that the Bush plan would give 43 percent of the benefits to the wealthiest 1 percent of taxpayers.

To this end, both Senate Minority Leader Tom Daschle and House Minority Leader Richard Gephardt joined forces to pull off a PR stunt on the Capitol Hill lawn with a sleek Lexus car on their side. They remonstrated that wealthy people who earn more than $300,000 per year will get a tax refund big enough to buy a Lexus while Joe Six-Pack gets back money enough to buy only a "muffler" on his used car.

For crying out loud, why, then, a Lexus, of all comparable cars of U.S. make available for this sound bite? Did it ever occur to those Democratic leaders that a Japanese auto company alone would benefit most from being given such a nice boost to publicity?

HARD TO BELIEVE THERE ARE ROLLING BLACKOUTS

(The State Journal-Register, April 6, 2001)

Who could have ever imagined hearing of rolling blackouts as often as we do in the America of the 21st century?

This sort of pitiful electric service may be something to be expected in a far-flung Third World country. But that's exactly what's happening in the Golden State, where the legendary Silicon Valley is located as the cradle of high tech.

Some say that California's energy crisis is just an aberration and won't affect the rest of the nation. However, others strongly argue that "when California sneezes, its neighbors catch cold." Disingenuously, politicians on the other side of the aisle would rather play a blame game.

Nonetheless, it doesn't take a rocket scientist to figure out the conundrum. For this past winter we also have seen our electric bills going through the roof. It simply boils down to a matter of supply and demand.

The Bush administration recently issued a timely warning that the spectre of another energy crisis looms large, given that we continue to depend heavily on imported oil with ever-decreasing domestic production and that we will soon enter the summer driving and cooling season.

As the old saying goes, forewarned is forearmed.

It's about time that we had a sound national energy policy in place to avert another round of energy crunch.

TO KNIT OR NOT

(Arthritis Today, March 7, 2002)

While deliberating the question "To knit or not" (Arthritis Today, March-April 2002). I can't help but take issue with the advice given to a patient with "arthritis in both hands that makes it difficult to do my favorite hobbies; knitting and embroidery." To begin with, we have seen an ever-increasing number of patients who end up with carpal tunnel syndrome following repetitive activities at home or in the pursuit of their recreational activities. Definitely, knitting or crocheting is considered one of the "culprits". Furthermore, medical literature is replete with articles where various authors have scientifically demonstrated that the median nerve in the carpal tunnel is being placed at undue risk during repetitive hand activities involving pinch or grasp.

Unfortunately, the questioner failed to give details on the type of her arthritis, whether it is rheumatoid or osteoarthritis, or simply one of the arthritic conditions such as trigger finger or tenosynovitis, etc. Nevertheless, it is common knowledge that arthritis in itself sometimes plays a pivotal role in carpal tunnel syndrome. Therefore, we are well advised to discourage any arthritic patients, young or old, from continuing to pursue their hobby of knitting and embroidery. It may be that "Hobbies make hands happy", but they are destined to make arthritic patients' lives unbearably miserable or utterly helpless.

NORTH KOREA DESERVES "AXIS OF EVIL" DESIGNATION

(The State Journal-Register, November 17, 2002)

Pyongyang's "bombshell" announcement that it keeps a secret weapons program shouldn't come as a big surprise.

It is a sad commentary on both South Korean President Kim's highfalutin' sunshine policy of engagement with the North and Uncle Sam's decade-long appeasement policy towards its nuclear blackmail.

Worse, the public has been duped into believing that the revised foreign policy of "carrot and no stick" would discourage a rogue regime from relentlessly pursuing its nuclear development.

What's even more shocking, Seoul has magnanimously rewarded Pyongyang with a bonanza of $1.3 billion in cash and goods as part of the sunshine policy of trying to encourage good will. To top it all off, Kim himself had made his bold yet exceedingly expensive junket to the North for an audience with his counterpart, Kim Jong II.

As German physician Norbert Vollersten, one of the few Westerners to travel without restriction in North Korea, reported earlier this year, "I soon realized that North Korea's starvation is not the result of natural disasters or even lack of natural resources. Like the Holocaust in Europe, the horror is man-made. Twenty-two million people suffer under a dictatorial regime that uses torture, surveillance and starvation as tools to control its own people. Only the regime's overthrow will end it."

Ironically, North Korea could pride itself upon achieving its nuclear capability and helping two presidents win Nobel Peace prizes.

Now, still any wonder why North Korea made the cut for President Bush's "axis of evil"?

JFK DOCTOR
UNFAIRLY MALIGNED

(The State Journal-Register, December 20, 2002)

Richard Reeves, in his recent column about "JFK's health secrets" (Nov 26), gave what's deemed an unsavory portrayal of Dr. Janet Travell "as a back specialist who nearly killed him (Kennedy) with indiscriminate injections of painkillers."

This harsh unfair critique wouldn't sit well with Dr. Travell's former students.

Being a distinguished professor of medicine at George Washington University School of Medicine, Dr. Janet Travell was named one of President Kennedy's personal physicians in the early '60s.

Even in her old age, the late Dr. Travell had tirelessly conducted numerous hands-on didactic seminars on management of myofascial pain syndrome, of which she was rightfully considered at the time the most renowned expert. I was fortunate enough to have been in one of her classes. Her mantra was detection of trigger points (TPS), spraying with vapocoolant and then sustained manual stretching of the affected muscles.

I still remember Dr. Travell as a very caring, gentle, extremely knowledgeable, meticulous yet very practical clinician and teacher.

In a nutshell, Dr. Travell is the epitome of a good, old-fashioned family physician.

One would be remiss if one fails to acknowledge that Dr. Janet Travell prescribed, of all remedies, a rocking chair for the 35th president's chronic back ailment.

Indeed, JFK sitting on his rocking chair is now the revered hallmark of his presidency.

JANET G. TRAVELL, M.D.

(1901-1997)

Dr. Janet G. Travell was born in New York, New York on December 17, 1901. She lived 95 remarkably productive years faithful to her often reported aphorisms: "Life is like a bicycle, you don't fall off until you stop pedaling." and "I'd rather rust out than wear out."

Her father John Williard Travell was a practicing physician for over 60 years (1870-1961) and he became one of the pioneer American physiatrists. His enthusiasm for life and medicine influenced both Janet and her sister Virginia to follow in his footsteps.

Dr. Travell received her undergraduate education from Wellesley College in 1922. She earned her M.D. degree in 1926 from Cornell medical College.

Dr. Travell married John Powell, an investment counselor in 1929. The marriage, which lasted until Mr. Powel's death in 1973, produced two daughters, Janet and Virginia. The personal aspects of Travell's life were as successful as her professional feats. She and her husband, Jack Powell, enjoyed a storybook romance.

Following her residency at New York Hospital, Dr. Travell was a research fellow at Bellevue Hospital. She then returned to Cornell and began work in the Dept. of Pharmacology as an instructor and later professor.

She became absorbed in the problem of skeletal muscle pain. She helped develop new anesthetic techniques for treating of painful muscle spasm by employing vapocoolant spray such as Ethanol Chloride. It was this pioneering expertise that changed her life in more ways than one.

In 1955 she was called upon by the Orthopedic Surgeon of the then Senator John F. Kennedy, who had failed to recover from major back surgeries he suffered in World War II.

Dr. Travell was able to locate muscular sources for his chronic pain, and injected low-level procaine directly into the Senator's lumbar muscles, which proved effective. She also discovered that one of Kennedy's legs was shorter than the other, and ordered special shoes to relieve the stress this condition put on his back.

Without the medical expertise of Dr. Travell, Kennedy and his family were convinced that his political career would have come to a premature end.

"I met John Kennedy in 1955 when he was the Junior Senator from Massachusetts", Travell would later recount. "He suffered greatly from war wounds and failed surgeries. When he first came to me he had been on crutches so long he had calluses under his arm pits."

In her 1968 autobiography, Travell also says she was 'tickled' on July 14, 1960 while she watched the formerly crippled Presidential candidate declare to a National TV audience that "the White House needs a young man of strength, health and vigor."

It would be no exaggeration to say that without Dr. Janet Travell, there would have been no President John F. Kennedy.

Once in the Oval Office, Kennedy picked Travell as his personal physician—the first woman "White House Physician." The anecdotal story has it that then-toddler John Kennedy, Jr. called Dr. Travell as "Toctor Tarbell." Dr. Travell served both Presidents Kennedy and Johnson, as well as their families by whom she was greatly appreciated and beloved. From 1961 to 1970 she also served

Associate Professor of Medicine, George Washington University Medical School.

It is Dr. Travell who introduced President Kennedy to the benefits of the old fashioned rocking chair, which then became an emblem of His Administration and had the effect of repopularizing rockers.

She authored more than 100 scientific articles and co-authored, with Dr. David G. Simons, "Myofascial Pain and Dysfunction; The Trigger Point Manual." This two-volume text is still revered as the "Red Bible."

Dr. Travell truly deserves being called "The Mother of Myofascial-Trigger Point Knowledge."

Chansoo Kim, M.D.

SOUTH KOREA STANDS
AT THE CROSSROADS

(The State Journal-Register, February 23, 2003)

On Dec. 19, 2002, South Korea held its presidential election. Someone aptly quipped about its outcome, "The North won."

Could anyone just shrug it off as kind of hyperbole? I guess not.

As Pyongyang escalates an unnerving game of its nuclear brinkmanship, we invariably notice a bizarre turn of events in Seoul that are utterly beyond our comprehension. For example, anti-American rallies reach a climax with U.S. flag burning in the street. Many South Koreans, particularly those young people born after the Korean War (1950-53) now fault the United States for the North's nuclear standoff.

It seems so obvious that they appear to embrace the communist North "more as a friend than an enemy" while ungratefully turning away from the United States, their savior and protector.

The radical new generation of Koreans may have little or no knowledge of the bloody war on the Korean Peninsula in which our country as its most stalwart ally paid an astounding price at the cost of 36,500 dead.

Which reminds me of an old Korean saying that "a day-old puppy isn't afraid of the tiger."

Nevertheless, Koreans, young and old, are well advised to always keep in mind that President Kim's Sunshine Policy of engagement has been a colossal failure. So is the 1994 peace agreement.

As things are now, South Korea stands at the crossroads. I, for one, hate to see her on the edge of the precipice.

GREAT AWAKENING

(2004 Lenten Devotional Booklet, First Christian Church,
March 14, 2004)

Mel Gibson's "The Passion of the Christ" finally debuted across the nation all at once on Ash Wednesday. What a timing it is as we observe Lent!

Certainly, this is not the time for finger pointing, but rather for genuine repentance, not only individually, but corporately as a nation.

The epic film may enable us to experience the vicarious crucifixion of Christ. However, some critics fretfully view "The Passion" as "having more power and gore than power and glory, more blood and guts than blood and redemption."

Let us turn to Isaiah 53:5-7 (NLV) "but he was wounded and crushed for our sins. He was beaten that we might have peace. He was whipped, and we were healed! All of us have strayed away like sheep. We have left God's path to follow our own. Yet the Lord laid on him the guilt and sins of us all. He was oppressed and treated harshly, yet he never said a word. He was led as a lamb to the slaughter and as a sheep is silent before the shearer, he did not open his mouth."

May this Lenten season usher in the Great Awakening for the 21st Century.

MR. REEVES,
THERE YOU HAVE IT

(The State Journal-Register, November 30, 2004)

President John F. Kennedy was assassinated over 41 years ago on November 22, 1963. According to an AP article published on November 22, 2004, personal memorabilia belonging to his favorite physician, the late Dr. Janet Travell, were recently sold at auction. The "Kennedy rocker", which Dr. Travell personally designed for the President, went for $11, 000. Other items sold for a tidy sum of money included her doctor's bag and an autographed copy of JFK's book "Profiles in Courage".

I feel I am compelled to revisit Richard Reeves' article "JFK's Health Secrets", which appeared in the State Journal Register on November 26, 2002. In his article, Mr. Reeves blatantly "blackballed" Dr. Travell as a "back specialist who nearly killed him with indiscriminate injections of pain killers." Nothing could be further from the truth. What a figment of Mr. Reeves' imagination! According to the AP article reporting the auction of Dr. Travell's belongings, President Kennedy once stated that Dr. Travell's treatments gave him "a new hope for a life free from crutches, if not from backache." Mr. Reeves, there you have it straight from the horse's mouth.

UPPER ROOM

(2005 Lenten Devotional Booklet, First Christian Church,
March 9, 2005)

"We know that in everything God works good with those who love him, who are called according to his purpose."—Romans 8-28 (RSV)

Several years ago, our Spiritual Ship abruptly suffered a shipwreck in the middle of its long voyage.

Being abandoned and forsaken, we were doomed to perish upon open seas. But miraculously we all survived the killer storms.

Now, who could have ever imagined that we would soon be called a Korean Christian church securely anchored in our Savior? How blessed we have been to hold worship services faithfully every Sunday at the Chapel, courtesy of the First Christian Church, our Benefactor.

Friends, behold the Chapel aloft, there we have our Upper Room. Dear Lord, this is our story and this is our song. We give our thanks for your unfailing love. We only praise your name to the skies.

STORY ABOUT RECOVERY SOMEWHAT MISLEADING

(The State Journal-Register, January 9, 2006)

The State Journal Register carried the front-page headline, "Waverly teen walks again—Rehab, braces help Rabon after experimental surgery." As I happen to be a rehabilitative medicine specialist (physiatrist), it sure grabbed my attention. But I find this "breathtaking" news at once baffling and misleading.

I say it is somewhat baffling in that Jacki Rabon could walk again only after the experimental surgery, and then with the aid of rehabilitation and braces as the headline clearly implies.

The story is also misleading because, in our rehabilitation practice, a young paraplegic, just like Jackie's case, can be trained through an intensive rehabilitation program to walk again with the leg braces and crutches, regardless of the experimental surgery or otherwise.

Nevertheless, what's more encouraging, being exceptionally disciplined and highly motivated at her tender age, Jackie may continue to make further progress with her rigid daily rehabilitation routine at home.

It is our fervent prayer and hope that the day will come soon when Jacki could walk again by herself and unassisted with the braces.

CARPAL TUNNEL SYNDROME A CONCERN FOR KNITTERS

(The State Journal-Register, January 28, 2006)

Due to the ever-increasing popularity in retro chic pastimes, it is reported there are now approximately 24 million active knitters and crocheters in the United States. This news is somewhat disturbing for the medical community.

I am not trying to throw cold water on some of the hobbies we all enjoy doing. But we know it as a fact that carpal tunnel syndrome (CTS) does often occur with pursuit of the popular hobbies, such as knitting, crocheting, sewing, gardening and even playing musical instruments. To cite one good example, the state of Maine has a high prevalence rate of CTS for its population. They have a long winter and some of the old folks just love to while away the time knitting and crocheting all winter long—even on a rocking chair. Yet, we do not hear a peep out of them, for it is all recreational.

On the other hand, if you recall, the former Oscar Mayer plant in Beardstown once shocked the nation with a torrent of CTS cases among its plant workers. They are vocational and work-related.

As far as the cumulative trauma disorders (CTDs) are concerned, it is common knowledge that recreational activities are just as important as the vocational factors. I still remember a witty remark by an old lady whose carpal tunnel syndrome was caused by her many years of knitting and crocheting: "Doctor, my hands sleep better than I do."

Knitting and crocheting may make you feel relaxed and may even be soothing, but your poor hands have to pay a hefty price for it. Be aware of the knitting bug!

FAITH, SCIENCE MIGHT HAVE MUCH IN COMMON

(The State Journal-Register, June 4, 2006)

The State Journal-Register editorial of May 19, "Faith, Science need not be at war," was at least a thought-provoking discourse.

At first blush, faith and science seem to be poles apart. Yet, with careful deliberation on the issue, we may realize that they have much in common. Let us take an airplane by way of illustration. We do not know diddly squat about its complicated aeronautics and we still keep flying every day without trepidation. There has to be a sort of faith in flight. The same goes for computers we work with or drugs we take as directed.

Now, back to religion, who has ever seen God? Scripture tells us that "faith is being sure of what we hope for and certain of what we do not see."

After all, what's more puzzling, "truth is stranger than fiction."

LETTER WRITER CONFUSES FAITH WITH TRUST

(The State Journal-Register, June 9, 2006)

Dear Editor,

Chansoo Kim, in a recent letter, made the argument that religion and science have much in common. This argument was then supported with the example that we have faith (religion) in air travel (science). It appears that Kim is confusing faith with trust.

Trust is based on belief in something because of past experience. We trust aeronautical science because we know, through past experience, that airplanes can and do fly safely.

Faith is based on belief in something with no evidence to support it and as such has no place in science. Religious people, on the other hand, regard faith as a positive virtue and may feel, paradoxically, that the less evidence there is the more virtuous their belief.

Science and religion are poles apart and will remain so until religion eliminates any claim that reliable knowledge can be obtained through revelation or divine authority; delete references to belief in supernatural beings or phenomena; and, finally, remove any claim of absolute truth.

George Free
Pleasant Plains

UNITED STATES
ENVY OF THE WORLD

(The State Journal-Register, June 22, 2006)

Nowadays, immigration is one of the hot-button issues facing the nation. About 12 million illegal aliens are reported to reside in the country and border security is being reinforced by National Guard deployment.

In his recent column, however, Richard Reeves opined, "it is a dangerous time to be American." Let us suppose for a moment that Uncle Sam changes its policy, opening the floodgates to accept say, 1 million people on a first come first served basis. Of course, all of them will be eligible to become U.S. citizens in due time.

Just picture in your mind the pandemonium caused by this blockbuster deal. "Miss Saigon" and its infamous helicopter hovering over the rooftop won't hold a candle to it. One question to Mr. Reeves and his soul mate French truck driver, in regard to those desperate immigrants, are they all plain loco, or just dimwits? Absolutely, not. They want badly to come here to seek what we call the American dream.

As long as we remain a superpower, we will be the envy of the world. And we have been and we also shall be vulnerable to barbarous terrorism. How could we ever forget the bloodcurdling 9/11 tragedy in 2001 and the disgraceful Iranian hostage crisis for 444 days from 11/4/79 to 1/20/81?

Mr. Reeves' French truck driver seems to be a case of sour grapes. He is just jealous of the American way of life and he is also hopelessly out of touch with reality.

After all, if France were one of our 50 states, it would be the fifth poorest in the land.

TOO MUCH IGNORANCE AND ARROGANCE FROM THE RIGHT

(The State Journal-Register, June 25, 2006)

Dear Editor,

Dr. Chansoo Kim's recent letter typifies much of what is wrong with our country. It's exactly that combination of right-wing ignorance and arrogance that makes us such a danger to the rest of the world.

Contrary to what Dr. Kim claims, recent polls suggest we are no longer envied by much of the world. In fact, the few countries that do envy us are among the most poor and least educated.

Dr. Kim also claims our superpower status has made us a target of terrorism. Virtually every country on the planet, regardless of military and/or economic strength, has, at one time or another, been the target of terrorism and, unfortunately, many will continue to be.

Dr. Kim doesn't want us to forget the bloodcurdling 9/11 tragedy or the disgraceful Iranian hostage crisis. Let's also not forget, among many other tragedies, the slaughter of Indians and theft of their lands, the enslavement of blacks, the support of past and present dictators and tyrants and the deaths of tens of thousands of innocent Iraqis. 9/11 was a tragedy, but it pales in comparison to those atrocities.

Dr. Kim also claims that Richard Reeves' French truck driver is hopelessly out of touch with reality. After all, he states, if France was one of the 50 states, it would be the fifth poorest in the land. That might be true, but it would also have one of the highest literacy rates, lowest infant mortality rates, highest life expectancies and be the only state with guaranteed health care for all its citizens.

Ray Hamilton
Gillespie

MISSIONARIES WILLING TO DIE FOR THEIR BELIEFS

(The State Journal-Register, August 22, 2007)

With the recent Korean hostage situation unfolding in Afghanistan, two conflicting views seem to prevail in the media. One view is that they strongly argue that the Korean missionary workers were simply naïve enough to bring disaster upon themselves while others simply condemn the lack of global outrage over the terrorists' heinous acts.

Out of the conundrum emerge revelations that South Koreas is second only to the U.S. in the number of missionaries they send abroad. As of last year, 16,600 Korean missionaries were stationed in 173 countries, including the Middle East, China and North Korea. In contrast, Korea has a population of 49 million and only about 30 percent of them are professing Christians.

Historically, a hundred years ago, both American and English mission teams had been sent out to the East, notably to China and Korea. During the Boxer Rebellion (1900) in China, foreign missionaries were targeted and many American missionary workers were martyred. Now the trend has been reversed—missionaries go from the East to the West.

As for these brave 23 Korean hostages, they are all devout young Christians in their 20s and 30s, and 17 of them are female nurses and English teachers. Two male team workers have already been murdered. They may be foolish in our eyes but their religious fervor is such that "The Great Commission" is something so noble or so sacred they must live by it and die for it, if necessary. They jumped into the lion's den, so to speak.

There is an old saying, "Man proposes and God disposes." "We know that in all things God works for the good of those who love him, who have been called according to his purpose."

ROH CHALLENGE TO BUSH
AT APEC WAS MISPLACED

(The State Journal-Register, September 21, 2007)

On the last day of the APEC meeting in Sidney, Australia, a brief yet snappy encounter was reported to have taken place between South Korean President Roh Moo Hyun and President Bush. Mr. Roh then demanded publicly that President Bush "declare the end of the Korean War and sign a peace pact with North Korea."

Nevertheless, Mr. Roh's call was surely misplaced at best. Instead, he should have challenged North Korean leader Kim Jon-Il to dismantle the nuclear facility and give up his relentless war mongering. Back in February, North Korea agreed to give up their entire program as well as to present a comprehensive list of their entire nuclear program and arsenal within 70 days. That was seven months ago.

Has Mr. Roh forgotten that Dictator Kim has already developed a nuclear bomb with its successful testing; and at his whim, he has been firing various ranges of missiles across the Korean Peninsula into the Sea of Japan. Furthermore, he once threatened to turn Seoul into "seas of fire" which makes us wonder whether Mr. Roh is losing his grip, thus tilting at the windmills.

FINANCIAL INDUSTRY FAILED TO LEARN ITS LESSON

(The State Journal-Register, December 1, 2007)

The financial industry has not learned its lesson from the savings-and-loan debacle in the 1980s. Any wonder history repeats itself?

Due to the current subprime mortgage crisis blowing up, the nation's economy is in such turmoil that the stock market "sinks in the tank" and the U.S. dollar seems to be in a freefall.

After all, they just may shrug it off as "the natural cycle of things."

But the fact is that banking giants and leading brokerage firms have all ditched "the old-fashioned way" for their ever-innovative gimmicks. They literally have been pushing the envelope all along.

Someone aptly remarked, "Wall Street shakes, twists, hammers on its innovations until they break and as long as the music plays, they love to dance."

Question of the day is, would bankers ever get away with making one major blunder after another?

One needs look no further than some of the pharmaceutical companies for what they have been going through!

To paraphrase the old saying, whoever has made up their bed, they have to sleep in it.

MORTGAGE BAILOUT PLAN NOTHING BUT POLITICS

(The State Journal-Register, December 26, 2007)

The subprime mortgage meltdown is slowly evolving at a glacial rate. Now the financial markets appear to have a serious problem with transparency.

In the beginning, there was a housing market boom of the century. It was red hot, so bankers, brokerage firms and mortgage brokers quickly jumped in with both feet and "head over heels."

Cash-rich predatory lenders began to lure potential homebuyers with the now infamous subprime loans and "teaser" rates. Some borrowers were highly speculative investors, living beyond their means, and others were "upgraders" and simply credulous homebuyers.

U.S. financiers literally bet the bank on this grandiose scheme of their own making. But when interest rates began to climb, many borrowers started defaulting, thus triggering a cascade of foreclosures nationwide, particularly in California, Nevada and Florida. One must ask where were the rating firms of Standard & Poor's and Moody's.

Now enters Uncle Sam with its rescue plan. This move is nothing but pure politics. With upcoming presidential and general elections, lawmakers on both sides of the aisle are eyeing to outdo each other with a more "juicy" or comprehensive bailout plan.

But it is worthwhile first to look at what happened to freezing wages and prices during the Nixon administration.

A bailout plan by any other name is still a bailout. The fact is that it will do more harm than good to the economy in the long run.

With federal intervention, "Prudence Rule" now takes a back seat to wildcat investing, hence unwittingly upholding "Moral Hazard" as a virtue.

CORN BELT IS JUST AS RELEVANT AS RUST BELT

(The State Journal-Register, January 16, 2008)

Syndicated radio talk show host Bill Press recently penned his column (Dec. 28), "Why so much say for Iowa?"

As usual, in his slanted piece, he challenged us with his signature rhetorical question, "Why? Why is Iowa still No. 1? And why do we still attach so much importance to a landlocked state that has so few voters, doesn't represent America, and is home to more pigs than people?"

I presume that Press meant it well, but that's where the rub is.

I have no idea how Iowans will take this blatant insult. They may just shrug it off like water off a duck's back. As an outsider, however, again, I feel somewhat offended by it.

Here is my bold response to Press' burning question.

Believe me or not, Iowa is still No. 1 as the nation's leading producer of corn, oats and soybeans, as well as hogs. Being part and parcel of the breadbasket, they are actually the backbone of our agribusiness.

Yes, Iowa is landlocked but 90 percent of its land is farmed. Press may not be aware that Iowans till the most fertile farmland of the country. Shall we call it "the land that flows with milk and honey"? How blessed we are!

I do believe that Iowa's farmers, though not so sophisticated as city folks, represent traditional American family values. They are God-fearing, hard-working, industrious, fair-minded and frugal people.

Politically speaking, the Corn Belt is just as relevant as the Rust Belt.

NEW HOPE FOR PEOPLE WITH CHRONIC PAIN

(The State Journal-Register, June 16, 2008)

As many as 10 million Americans may have fibromyalgia, which is a chronic pain syndrome marked by widespread aches, stiffness, fatigue, trouble sleeping and cognitive dysfunction known as "fibro-fog."

In the 1950s, fibromyalgia has been called fibrositis in the Rheumatology Primer. In 1990, the American College of Rheumatology, or ACR, established diagnostic criteria based on the scoring system of 18 potential tender points in the body. Current research findings clearly point to a neurologic disorder of central pain processing. Thus, patients with fibromyalgia experience a heightened sensitivity to pain with dysfunction in their pain-killing mechanism.

Now, some clinical researchers even go so far as to claim that fibromyalgia is not a rheumatologic disease anymore. Furthermore, the medical community also tends to view fibromyalgia as the prototypical central pain disorder.

Along with non-pharmacologic approaches, two main promising drug classes of interest are available: (1) dual receptor reuptake inhibitors (anti-depressants) like duloxetine (Cymbalta) and (2) anti-epileptic drugs like pregabalin (Lyrica). So far, Lyrica is the first and only drug approved by the FDA for the treatment of fibromyalgia. Clinically, Lyrica has shown remarkable efficacy.

Therefore, with the new insights and therapies on the horizon, much needed help is finally on the way, and physicians will no longer need to refer fibromyalgia patients to the rheumatologist.

GLOBALIZATION AFFECTING HEALTH CARE, TOO

(The State Journal-Register, July 14, 2008)

We make it almost a national pastime to blame outsourcing for job losses. Now add this equation to the rapidly growing medical tourism in our country.

It used to be that many foreigners and their dignitaries have traveled to the USA to seek the expertise and advanced technology available in leading medical centers. The trend has now reversed; in this era of the global village we live in, like anything else, the health-care market also undergoes globalization with cutthroat competition.

According to the most reliable sources, 750,000 Americans are estimated to seek offshore medical care this year. The medical procedures for which they pursue medical tourism cover practically the whole spectrum of medicine, namely from bariatric surgery, cosmetic and plastic surgery, coronary bypass, total knee and hip replacement, fertilization treatment to organ transplantation, particularly stem cell therapy for incurable neurological conditions and spinal cord injuries.

Overseas hospitals also pull out all the stops to woo American patients by offering their "cheap" medical services. The cost is supposed to be a "fraction" of that in the U.S. even after factoring in expenses of travel and accommodations.

Worse yet, the insurance industry has become an active participant in medical tourism, working on the feasibility of outsourcing expensive medical procedures to offshore healthcare destinations.

As medical tourism continues to grow and thrive, we urge the AMA to look into this most unsettling issue and come up with a comprehensive policy on medical tourism to ensure safety and quality of the care rendered overseas.

In the meantime, prospective medical tourists, be aware! You get what you pay for.

CAN SEE NO LIGHT AT END OF THE CREDIT CRISIS TUNNEL

(The State Journal-Register, August 30, 2008)

The U.S. credit crisis is now a year old since we went through a "financial Katrina." Yet, we see no light at the end of the tunnel, despite Uncle Sam's $170 billion stimulus package earlier this year and the Federal Reserve's aggressive interventions.

Indeed, the current outlook of our economy still appears so gloomy that Congress is already talking about the urgent need of another bailout plan.

We are told that subprime mortgage defaults put us into this financial abyss. But strangely enough, we now begin to hear more subprime deterioration due to rising default rates among the wealthy, so-called superprime borrowers. They have enjoyed a decade of easy money and rising asset values. Like everyone else, the wealthy didn't expect the party to end.

The bottom line is that poor middle-class taxpayers are all caught between a rock (subprime) and a hard place (superprime). I wonder if this emerging superprime specter might be the last straw.

LPGA'S ENGLISH
EDICT IS OUTRAGEOUS

(The State Journal-Register, October 14, 2008)

It seems that the LPGA has just revealed her "worse half" with the recent announcement of English proficiency as part of the eligibility requirements.

Specifically, the new policy demanded that "all who have been on Tour for two years must pass an oral evaluation of their English skills. Failure would result in suspended membership."

This outrageous edict was unquestionably intended to discriminate, if anything, against a certain ethnic group.

We know that the LPGA has 121 international players from 26 countries and 45 of them are from South Korea, representing a sizable number of tour members. Once, a pioneer Korean woman golfer even quipped, tongue-in-cheek, that "it is going to be the Korean Tour pretty soon." Also, it's a fact that Korean women golfers have made their presence known in the golf tournaments by winning many championships.

Needless to say, sportsmanship has nothing to do with an athlete's ability to speak English but has everything to do with his or her athletic performance and skills.

Just for argument's sake, let us take Major League Baseball (MLB). We have quite a few foreign players in both the National and American Leagues. How often we admire their awesome skills being demonstrated on the field? What about a rookie outfielder from Japan who made it to the All-Star game this summer? Who cares about their English proficiency off the field, as long as they can play outstanding games on the field? We have yet to hear from the baseball Commissioner about the players' English requirement.

Had the LPGA not rescinded their bigoted policy, it would be known as, to quote cartoonist Chris Britt, the "Ladies Prejudiced Golf Association."

A LONG WAY TO GO IN
SPINAL INJURY TREATMENT

(The State Journal-Register, February 17, 2009)

A new era of human embryonic stem cell therapy dawns on us with the FDA's recent approval.

This watershed event can be hailed as the greatest news for spinal cord injury victims. This reminds us painfully of several young people in the community who desperately went overseas to seek stem cell transplant.

Geron Corp., one of the United States' leading biotechnology companies, was given a green light to conduct the first clinical trial with stem cell therapy. The initial study will target a select group of complete paraplegics. However, transplants will be undertaken seven to 14 days after the spinal cord injury. The "window of opportunity" is rather short and time-sensitive. The research study aims to prove both the safety and effectiveness of stem cell therapy.

Even if the clinical trial succeeds, as expected, it will be years before stem cell therapies are approved and become widely available to spinal cord injury patients.

As Dave Bakke eloquently pointed out in his gripping story about John Link, "The mind is a powerful ally." The old adage of "sound mind in the sound body" wouldn't apply to a quadriplegic patient like John.

HEAVEN'S GREATEST DELIGHTS

(Our Daily Bread, RBC Ministry, July 8, 2009)

Read: Revelation 22:1-5

"Eye has not seen, nor ear heard . . . the things which God has prepared for those who love Him."—1 Corinthians 2:9

What will be one of heaven's supreme joys?

Joni Eareckson Tada, disabled as a teenager in a diving accident, has been a paraplegic for over 40 years. One would imagine that her greatest longing would be the ability to walk, even run, free from the confinement of her wheelchair.

But Joni tells us that her greatest desire is to offer a "praise that is pure." She explains: "I won't be crippled by distractions, or disabled by insincerity. I won't be handicapped by a ho-hum half-heartedness. My heart will join with yours and bubble over with effervescent adoration. We will finally be able to fellowship fully with the Father and the Son. For me, this will be the best part of heaven."

How that speaks to my divided heart and grips my unfocused spirit! What a blessing to offer "a praise that is pure," with no wandering thoughts, no self-centered requests, no inability to soar above my earth-bound language!

In heaven, "there shall be no more curse, but the throne of God and of the Lamb shall be in it, and His servants shall serve Him" (Rev. 22:3). May the prospect of heaven enable us to experience a foretaste of that God-glorifying worship even here and now.

Vernon Grounds

HEAVEN'S GREATEST DELIGHTS

(Our Daily Bread, RBC Ministry, July 8, 2009)

I have been a faithful reader of Our Daily Bread for many years. While doing our family devotion this morning on 7/8/09, we came across what obviously seems to be a factual error: Ms. Joni Tada is a quadriplegic, not a paraplegic. Diving accident always causes a horrible injury to the cervical spine, thus rendering the victim a quadriplegic. In my specialty of Rehab Medicine, there is a huge difference between paraplegics and quadriplegics, almost like day and night, in terms of activities of daily living (ADL) and assistance. Be that as it may, Joni is highly regarded as a spiritual role model among believers across the nation and beyond.

Editor's Reply

Dear Chansoo:

Thank you for your e-mail. We appreciate your careful reading and your taking the time to write us about our mistake about Joni who is a quadriplegic.

We apologize for this mistake.

Thanks again.

Sincerely,
Anne Cetas
Managing Editor
Our Daily Bread

DOESN'T UNDERSTAND FDA APPROVAL OF BOTOX

(The State Journal-Register, April 8, 2010)

Recently, the Food and Drug Administration approved Botox for elbow, wrist and finger spasms. The news is baffling and enigmatic to the medical community.

The new policy directive calls for a critical review and possible revision, lest the FDA should give Botox a "blanket clearance" for such garden-variety ailments as hand spasms, stiffness and tightness, etc.

For starters, spasms and spasticity are two distinct medical terms and should not be used interchangeably. Spasm is defined in Dorland's Medical Dictionary as "a sudden, violent, involuntary contraction of a muscle or a group of muscles, attended by pain and interference with function." Spasms are localized and temporary in nature. The case in point is back spasms we've all experienced sometime in our lives.

Spasticity is caused by the irreversible underlying central nervous system disorders such as stroke, cerebral palsy, traumatic brain injury, etc. The affected patients develop spasticity predominantly in the flexor muscles of the upper extremity and extensors in the lower extremity. On the contrary, hand spasms and tightness are commonly encountered in cases of hand overuse syndrome, tenosynovitis, carpal tunnel syndrome, rheumatoid arthritis and osteoarthritis.

Conventional treatment of those medical conditions has been local rest and oral analgesics coupled with applications of appropriate physical modality. This simple yet effective therapeutic approach is more than sufficient. Of all things, why Botox now? Certainly, the risk outweighs the temporary benefit.

BTX-A or Botox is the potent neurotoxin produced by the anaerobic bacillus clostridium and causes paralysis of the injected muscles at the neuromuscular junction. Botox invariably requires repeated injections, as its effect wears off over time. Based on my personal clinical experiences with moderately severe spastic hemiplegics and quadriplegics, Botox injection has not been as effective or useful as claimed to be, particularly for the spastic hand.

NOTHING, NOT EVEN QUILTING, IS FREE OF RISK

(The State Journal-Register, June 1, 2010)

Everything involves some risk in life and nothing is perpetually "all fun." Quilting is no exception, though it could be a most relaxing recreation or "therapy" for some people.

The fact is that cumulative trauma disorder or carpal tunnel syndrome is often caused by our pursuit of common recreation activities such as quilting, crocheting or knitting, etc.

In 1992, the Mayo Clinic published a provocative article in which they found a higher incidence of CTS in the retirement community than in the work force.

To put it another way, recreational activities are just as important as the vocational factors in the causation of CTS. If ever combined, they would make for the worst case scenario.

In my practice, I have had some quilters and crocheters as patients and I found them to be "nice folks," trying to shrug off their persistent hand pain as a "nuisance." However, I bet my bottom dollar that a 14-year veteran of quilting is bound to have electrodiagnostic evidence of CTS, regardless of symptoms.

From a medical perspective, long-term quilting is hazardous to health, playing havoc with your hands.

MOTIVATION, DISCIPLINE NEEDED TO FIGHT OBESITY

(The State Journal-Register, August 21, 2010)

Medicine is so highly specialized that "new subspecialties" are being called into action to meet our changing medical needs. Notably, they are fitness medicine, holistic medicine, alternative medicine, let alone pain medicine, geriatric medicine and sports medicine.

Nowadays, the public is literally deluged with a flood of the latest medical developments and therapeutics. It's only a click away. We can look up on any topic without bothering to consult a medical text.

Yet, obesity in both adults and children still remains a grave threat to our national health care. Obviously, no amount of medical information and recommended physical activity programs would ever put a dent in the horrendous problem of obesity control.

Parenthetically, I have made some interesting personal observations. In our neighborhood, we watch some of the people take a walk regularly in the morning and alas, we always come across the same familiar faces. I have yet to see an overweight person join us in the walk.

More often than not, at the workplace, there lies on the table mouth-watering glazed doughnuts. They disappear in no time, like "hot cakes." Who isn't tempted? Indeed, we are what we eat.

When it comes to a drastic change of one's lifestyle, what it takes more than anything else is motivation, discipline and compliance. As the old adage goes, "You can lead a horse to water but you can't make it drink."

SURPRISED PAGE NOT SEEN AS MEAN-SPIRITED

(The State Journal-Register, September 16, 2010)

In this day and age of racial tension smoldering in our country, Clarence Page boldly opines in his recent column that there is "a place for Ebonics speakers after all" at the Drug Enforcement Agency. Ebonics or jive is spoken mostly by black people in America and is also known as "Black English."

Somehow, Page attempts to unwittingly tie in all black people with drug trafficking or drug crimes in Chicago and Baltimore, among other major cities in the nation. Just as it takes one to know one, so "it takes Ebonics to catch drug dealers."

Unfortunately, the drug culture permeates our current society as a whole and no particular ethnic group or race could claim immunity from the darn sickness. The DEA may be able to win a battle in the street but they still could lose a major drug war escalating along the Mexican border.

The article in question, if it ever were penned by someone other than Clarence Page, would surely have been castigated for being "mean spirited" or even "bigotry". Most likely, the media would weigh in on the issue, throwing the poor guy under the bus.

This reminds us of the old adage, "The road to hell is paved with good intentions."

DON'T FORGET CARTER'S LANDMARK LEGISLATION

(The State Journal-Register, October 28, 2010)

Kathleen Parker provides for the public several takeaways from the documentary film "Inside Job."

She starts off with her talking points: "One, trying to assign blame to either Democrats or Republicans is pointless. Everyone is culpable. From the early 1980's when Ronald Reagan deregulated banks, through the two Bushes, Bill Clinton and now Barack Obama, each administration has endorsed—and each Congress has helped tweak—laws and rules that made systematic abuses and the meltdown not only possible but, looking back, inevitable."

However, Parker clearly failed to evoke here the very important name of Jimmy Carter, who signed in 1977 his landmark legislation into the law. The Community Re-Investment Act was designed to encourage commercial banks and savings associations to meet the needs of mid—and low-income neighbors, specifically prohibiting a practice known as "redlining." Over the years, the CRA has undergone some revisions and changes, evidently for the worse. It does not take a PhD in economics to figure out how the whole financial system has run amok; banks were lending 110 percent of the purchase price with no down payment.

Nevertheless, Congress turned its blind eye to the cancerous outgrowth of Fannie Mae and Freddie Mac. Just before the meltdown, things got so bad that the nationally renowned financial advisor Malcolm Berko, in a recent column, still pokes fun at the banking corruption. To quote him, "At some banks, a beagle could borrow $300,000 using its dog tag ID as a Social Security number."

In retrospect, the Community Re-investment Act is believed to have played no small role in the worst financial crisis since the Great Depression.

FLAWED LOGIC USED IN LEAF PICKUP EDITORIAL

(The State Journal-Register, November 26, 2010)

I have to take issue with the State Journal-Register's Nov. 10 editorial in regard to the leaf issue.

Needless to say, we are in financially very difficult times nationally as well as locally. Belt-tightening or fiscal conservatism is a must and should be on the top of our priority list. Therefore, the city's move to shorten the free leaf pickup period is more than justified under the circumstances. There is no argument there.

However, what I have to complain about is its flawed logic: "Those with large yards are the ones most likely able to afford the stickers that will be required for collection of bagged leaves after the free period."

Yet, the size of one's yard, or house for that matter, has virtually nothing to do with the amount of leaves to be collected. Rather, house location—open or secluded—and the number and kind of trees in the neighborhood and even the unpredictable wind factor all have everything to do with annoying piles of leaves on the ground.

Nature has no consideration for the rich or the poor. More often than not, we also need indirect help or cooperation from our neighbors.

N. KOREA HAS ODD WAY
OF REPAYING GOOD WILL

(The State Journal-Register, December 15, 2010)

South Korea has been brutally attacked twice this year by ever belligerent North Korea.

On March 26, a North Korean submarine apparently launched a torpedo attack, killing 46 sailors. It was barely eight months before North Korean troops again bombarded the same Yeonpyeong Island. This time they fired mercilessly upon the defenseless islanders, killing two marines, several civilians and wounding more than a dozen people.

However, for the first time in three years since President Lee Myong-Bak, a conservative, came to power, his government sent to North Korea its unusually generous food aid for their flood victims: 5,000 tons of rice was shipped out on Oct. 28.

Yet, the North brazenly opted to repay this good will with rocket firings. Even a dog, it is said, does not bite the hand that feeds him.

In order to understand how we have come to such an impasse with North Korea, it is essential that we revisit some of the watershed events that took place over the past 20 years.

First and foremost, there have been two major inter-Korean summit meetings in the last decade between the leaders of both Koreas. Former President Kim Dae Jung (1998-2003) gave billions of dollars of aid and trade to the communist North under that grand name of the "Sunshine Policy." He also made a record-breaking junket to Pyongyang in June 2000 and reportedly paid a stiff price of $500 million just for the visit with Kim Jong II.

Ironically, he won a Nobel Peace Prize for his "bold" move. His successor, President Roh Moo-Hyun (2003-08), once a radical left activist, followed in his mentor's footsteps, carrying the torch for the Sunshine Policy of engagement with the North. Roh also made his trip in 2007 to meet with Kim Jong II. This decade-long sunshine policy toward Pyongyang is now believed to have played a pivotal role in helping North Korea become a full fledged nuclear power in 2006.

Furthermore, we also have more than enough blame to go around. The United States has its own share. Among other things, the Bill Clinton/Jimmy Carter "Agreed Work" deal in 1994 lets North Korea "freeze" plutonium production in exchange for oil, construction of two light water nuclear power plants and five years' reprieve of U.N. inspection. This has been a colossal blunder on our part.

All these years we have been feeding a grizzly bear, so to speak. Now, being armed with weapons of mass destruction, North Korea is undertaking dangerous and provocative attacks to challenge our collective will.

Email Response

N. KOREA HAS ODD WAY OF REPAYING GOOD WILL

(The State Journal Register, December 15, 2010)

Kindness is often times viewed as weakness. Not only that, but when kindness is extended for great lengths of time, regardless of behavior, it is no longer thanked. It becomes expected and demanded and if denied or not increased on demand, belligerence often results. You bet DPRK is doing exactly that, Chansoo, so too is this sentiment displayed right here in our own country where domestic affairs are concerned—see unemployment or even illegal aliens—subjects for evidence of it . . .

We can also look to untold billions sent to African nations or even Southeast Asia in the form of "aid" and they are no better off today for it. Dependency has resulted instead of prosperity. As an addict's fiend, their behavior becomes more and more aggressive and yes, dangerous.

If China wants to use DPRK as a proxy, not unlike the way Iran uses Syria. Hezbollah and Hamas (not to mention the Palestinian people themselves), then the right way to address that is for the international community to see China be the lone actor doing so. In this way, obscureknight's post supports Chansoo's message that the Carter and Clinton path, the progressive path of appeasement, is, in fact, a colossal mistake. Well done, obscureknight. Great Letter, Chansoo.

ZMK25

CORE VALUES VS ECONOMY

(The State Journal-Register, January 9, 2011)

I just can't let Mary Sanchez's column (1/3/11) get by me without making a comment on it. Indeed she has raised some provocative thoughts on the weighty issues of marriage, poverty and economics.

In regards to the Heritage Foundation's upcoming report that "the collapse of marriage is the major cause of poverty," Sanchez strongly counters that the Foundation's "bold statement" is nothing but the Conservative Movement's old tired ploy to push their own agenda. In the same breath, she goes on to say that "marriage is a good thing. Children with married parents do benefit—if the marriage is emotionally healthy and free from domestic violence, addictions and emotional trauma."

Unfortunately, our good old traditional family and moral values have steadily declined over the decades. As a result, the divorce rate is skyrocketing, so is the number of single parent homes with deadbeat Dads. Nevertheless, marriage, poverty and economics are so correlated that once the chain is broken, it sets a vicious cycle in motion.

Let me further elaborate on it with a few good examples. 1) From some of our Depression Era folks, we still hear about their heartwarming and invigorating stories on how much they struggled as a family to survive single-handedly, even without our current social programs. Their generation emerged from the Depression stronger than ever. 2) As for the 38th President Gerald R. Ford, when he was 2 years old, his parents were divorced and his mother remarried and the Elder Ford adopted him into the family. 3) President Barack Obama was abandoned by his biological father. Yet he has become the most powerful leader in the world. What a good role model he is for children from single parent homes not only here but the world over.

In order to build a strong society, we have to further strengthen and reinforce our ever fragile family system with the kind of love and commitment as exchanged in the solemn wedding vow. This urgent task is just as critical as our much desired economic stability, for they are two cornerstones of our foundation.

NEWER CONCEPT OF STROKE REHABILITATION

(The State Journal-Register, February 21, 2011)

Thanks to recent advances in both medical and preventive care, stroke is no longer the third most common cause of death in U.S. It gives way to chronic lower respiratory diseases. Also, stroke rehabilitation has come a long way the past several decades.

As a specialist, I can't help but to comment on the Journal's "study of stroke rehab." (2/14/11). Once the brain is injured by a stroke or trauma, its damaged part never regenerates but is strongly believed to retain the capacity to reorganize or repair itself over time by forming new neural connections with the surrounding neurons and axonal sprouting. This neurological repair process is called neuroplasticity, or brain malleability. Thus, the prevailing new concept of neuroplasticity has helped Rehab medicine to drastically change their approaches to treatment modality and direction. Recovery after a brain injury takes place in two main stages: their first stage is called Spontaneous reorganization and the second stage is Training-induced recovery phase. Spontaneous reorganization after a stroke typically plateaus about 3 months after insult, whereas spontaneous recovery after the traumatic brain injury is found to plateau about 6 months after injury. Therefore, a 3 to 6 months time frame was felt to be the critical period for optimal rehab. Yet, training–induced neural plastic changes are not found to be time-sensitive like the initial stage of Spontaneous reorganization. That's when the widely accepted and popular constraint-induced movement therapy (CIMT) comes into play. The focus of constraint-induced therapy lies with forcing the patient to use the affected limb by restraining the unaffected or normal limb. Years ago, it used to be the other way around. Most stroke patients tend to stop using the affected limb because they are naturally discouraged by the difficulty. As a result, a process called "Learned non-use" sets in, furthering deterioration. By having the patient to continue to be engaged in the repetitive exercises with the affected limb, we try to help the brain to grow new neural pathways. For that very reason, regardless of whether high-tech or low-tech, simply continuation of long-term maintenance home therapy is extremely beneficial to the stroke and TBI victims, for neuroplasticity plays a key role in their eventual recovery. Any wonder why "longer therapy and more therapy is best."

WHAT IS CARTER THINKING?

(The State Journal-Register, May 17, 2011)

Former President Jimmy Carter has caused quite a stir in Seoul with his recent trip to North Korea. He is known pejoratively as "Pyongyang's mouthpiece."

True enough, he issued an incredibly off-the-wall and over-the-top statement that "both South Korea and the U.S. should be held responsible for worsening starvation in the North, for they deliberately withhold food aid to the North Koreans purely for political and military reasons."

For crying out loud, where's Carter's outrage when the North viciously attacked South Korea, though unprovoked, twice last year, first blowing up a South Korean warship by a torpedo and then later firing upon the Yeonpyung Island to kill innocent people.

The Obama administration also refuses to consider giving any food assistance under the circumstances, unless they refrain from their hostile acts. According to one of the leading newspapers in Seoul, Kim Jong Il had a French veterinarian flown in just to take care of his own pets (dogs and horses) and his heir apparent is building a huge mansion in their capital, once again flaunting to the world their absolute, corrupt power and ill-gotten wealth all the while their poor people are starving to death.

Some politicians and pundits claim that Carter has been the worst president in U.S. history, but we have to leave that matter up to the historians. Yet, Carter often gets to be so officious in our foreign affairs that even his stature as ex-president might be adversely affected.

EMAIL RESPONSES TO:
WHAT IS CARTER THINKING?

North Korea and North Korea alone is responsible for its starving people. There is no reason for anyone to go hungry. Carter likes to blame everyone for everyone's plight. And in my opinion he is probably the worst President of that latter half of the 20th Century.

Frank Roosevelt

Clark—"Jimmy is ramping up his activity levels, for fear of being outpaced by Obama as our country's 'Worst President.'
Yeah, yeah . . . I'll bet you're right on, on this one . . .
Statements like this are why people ignore even the true and factual statements you make . . . worldwide

Anonymous

HAPHAZARD USE OF "REHAB"

(The State Journal-Register, June 17, 2011)

Columnist Ruth Marcus is spot-on when she gets highly critical of "rehab" as an all-purpose excuse or "Laundromat." She even deplores that ours has become "a nation of rehab" and "we live in an age of rehab as reality shows."

Several decades ago, rehab, short for rehabilitation, used to be an arcane word and now it is a highly popular buzzword, although much abused and self-serving. The word is thrown around haphazardly and even disgracefully.

Dorland's Medical Dictionary, however, defines rehab as the restoration of an ill or injured patient to self-sufficiency or gainful employment at his highest attainable skills. Rehab invariably involves helping the disabled person to retrain and to relive with what he is left with.

My mentor, Dr. Howard Rusk, Founder of Rehab Medicine, used to remind us that "rehab adds years to life and life to years."

One's tedious journey to rehab is always regarded as noble, uplifting and rewarding adventure. Being a rehab specialist, I won't begrudge any afflicted person the benefit of his own rehab effort, but individuals with self-destructive and shameful addiction problems may require a remedial type of rehab by way of professional counseling, therapy and psychiatric treatment. Just as we have a military school for troubled teens, we may need to have a special rehab school for troubled adults and not at an undisclosed place.

HAPHAZARD USE OF "REHAB"

I believe that rehab is a place where people who want help with their problems go to get help. Too often it seems that celebrities and public figures use rehab as a sort of 'reset button' to get forgiveness for their wrong doings. It's being used as a sort of confession to wipe away their sins . . . when they don't believe they have sinned at all.—Ashrak

Jails are all about rehabilitation these days . . . right? Is this a place "where people who want help with their problems go to get help?"

Additionally, judges are nowadays assigning forced "rehabilitation" as part of sentencing . . . correct?

Something doesn't quite fit here . . . does it?

In my opinion, many of today's 'rehabilitation centers' amount to little more than yesteryear's reeducation camps.

Can rehab be a good thing? Absosmurfly! But that is only the case when it is a tool used by folks who do want help themselves. When government compels it, the key component is missing—the willingness of the individual to help themselves.—Anonymous

There is nothing wrong for going to rehab if one has serious issues. But every time I turn around we are coming up with a new problem. Depression is a term that is thrown around too carelessly. I have never met a depressed person who has clearly defined written down goals.

We have become so reliant upon the collective that we have lost our individual drive. Individuals are what drive this country, not the collective. But the collective agenda has made many weak-minded people out there. Yes, some rehab is necessary, but individual drive and determination is the best medicine.—stickman4077

June 7
Tuesday

God Is God

READ:
Daniel 3:8-30

Women received their dead raised to life again. Others were tortured, not accepting deliverance, that they might obtain a better resurrection.
—Hebrews 11:35

THE BIBLE IN ONE YEAR:
2 Chronicles 28–29
John 17

When Polycarp (AD 69–155), who was bishop of the church at Smyrna, was asked by Roman authorities to curse Christ if he wanted to be released, he said, "Eighty-six years I have served Him, and He never did me any wrong. How can I blaspheme my King who saved me?" The Roman officer threatened, "If you do not change your mind, I will have you consumed with fire." Polycarp remained undaunted. Because he would not curse Christ, he was burned at the stake.

Centuries earlier, when three young men named Shadrach, Meshach, and Abed-Nego faced a similar threat, they answered, "O Nebuchadnezzar, . . . our God whom we serve is able to deliver us from the burning fiery furnace, and He will deliver us from your hand, O king. But if not, let it be known to you, O king, that we do not serve your gods" (Dan. 3:16-18). A similar experience but two different outcomes. Polycarp was burned alive, but Shadrach, Meshach, and Abed-Nego left the furnace unsinged.

Two different results but the same display of faith. These men showed us that faith in God is not simply faith in what God can do. But it's the belief that God is God whether He delivers us or not. He has the final say. And it's our decision to choose to follow Him through it all. —Albert Lee

Lord, help us trust You all the time
Regardless of what comes our way,
Accepting from Your goodness that
You always have the final say. —Sper

Life is hard, but God is good—all the time.

God Is God—June 7

DEATH OF ST. POLYCARP

Letter to Managing Editor:

This is in regards to the June 7th devotional in which "Polycarp was burned alive". I believe that nothing could be further than that from the truth. The fact is St. Polycarp was rather stabbed to death when he was miraculously spared by the flames that just swirled around him, not even touching his body.

Smyrna, also known as the church of St. Polycarp still stands tall as a living testimonial to his unblemished faithfulness to our Risen Lord, and to the glory of God.

Years ago, I was fortunate enough to take a group tour of Seven Churches in Asia Minor (Turkey). Is there any wonder why Smyrna remains the only surviving of the Seven Churches in Revelation?!

Please note that I have e-mailed several times to Our Daily Bread about the gross misrepresentation of St. Polycarp. As of this date, you remain silent for some unknown reasons.

Editor's Response: Polycarp's Death—July 6, 2011

Dear Dr. Kim,

I am not aware of a tradition that claims that Polycarp had to be stabbed to death because he was unaffected by flames. There may be such a tradition, but it isn't corroborated, as far as I know, by the writing of the church fathers.

Dan Vander Lugt

Letter to Editor: Polycarp's Death—July 6, 2011

To say the least, I am flabbergasted to receive an evasive reply in a month's time since I emailed the managing Editor on 6/7/11 when I came across a gross misrepresentation of St. Polycarp's death. I just wonder if you have been to Smyrna church. I do not understand what you mean by a tradition. What tradition makes you convinced that St. Polycarp was burned alive. I am much concerned about your obvious attempt to cover up or to pull the wool over my eyes. You will not be able to pull it off. May I refer you to "The life and Martydom of St. Polycarp." I myself have a brochure of Smyrna church I brought with me when I visited it some years ago. On the wall inside the church, there is a huge mural showing Polycarp's death. You mean to tell me that they are spreading around misinformation to the believers the world over. You have my assurance that I will pursue this grave issue at all my costs. This will be my last communication to you and RBC.

Editor's Response: Polycarp's Death—July 7, 2011

Dear Christian Friend,

I'm sorry it took some time to respond to your email. I'm the person who normally responds to questions relating to church history, and I was on vacation.

Didn't mean to give you an evasive reply. I simply have never heard that Polycarp died the way you described. I trust that you are aware that local traditions often don't have a solid historical basis.

If you are aware of any mention of Polycarp's death by stabbing in the writing of the church fathers, I would be interested.

Meanwhile, your characterization of our mention of Polycarp's death as a "gross misrepresentation" seems extreme.

Dan Vander Lugt

Smirne, Turkey Response—August 24, 2011

Dear Mr. Chansoo Kim,

Sorry for my English.

I'm Fr. Marco Dondi, Chancellor of the Archdiocese of Izmir, Turkey. I write you in the name of Archbishop S.E. Mons. Ruggero Franceschini about the letter you addressed him concerning the death of our saint.

You are absolutely right: St. Polycarp was stabbed, as the flames couldn't affect him. **This is the only tradition** of the Church, attested by the *Martyrium Polycarpi,* written before 200 A.C., few years after his death. The text, (letter of the Church of Izmir to the Church of Filomelio) is considered among the first examples of martyr-literature in Christian history.

Anyway, don't waste your time in pursuing this thing, it's an error, not a "gross misrepresentation." Tell them kindly to read the *Martyrium,* and I think they will apologize.

If you want you can forward this mail to them.

Thank you for your love towards our great saint, pray for this little church and may St. Polycarp bless you.

Fr. Marco Dondi

Chansoo Kim, M.D.

Our Daily Bread, Editor's Response—August 25, 2011

Dear Chansoo Kim,

Thanks for sharing this with me.

I stand corrected!

Dan Vander Lugt (ODB)

Our Daily Bread, Editor's Response—September 13, 2011

Dear Mr. Kim,

Thanks for forwarding the information from Fr. Dondi.

I wasn't aware of this tradition, as it wasn't mentioned in any of my sources.

I'm grateful to know about it, and am glad to have my mistake pointed out.

I'll save Fr. Dondi's response for any future letters on this subject.

I'm glad that you followed through on this.

Dan Vander Lugt (ODB)

DEATH OF ST. POLYCARP

SAINT POLYCARP WAS <u>NOT</u> BURNED ALIVE

- St. Polycarp lived in about 69-155 A.D., and was the Bishop of Smyrna, Izmir in modern Turkey. He was the leading Christian figure in Roman Asia Minor.

- Polycarp was a disciple of St. John the Apostle.

- As they were about to nail Polycarp, he said: "Let me be as I am; for He who makes it possible for me to endure the fire will also make it possible for me to remain on the pyre unmoved without the security of nails." Thus, they only bound him, but did not nail him. Polycarp looked up to heaven and said this last prayer: *"Lord God Almighty, Father of Your Beloved and Blessed Son Jesus Christ, through whom we have received knowledge of You, God of angels and powers and every created thing and all the race of the just who dwell before You. I bless You because You have considered me worthy of this day and hour to receive a portion among the number of martyrs in the Cup of your Christ unto the resurrection of eternal life, both of soul and body in the incorruption of the Holy Spirit. May I be received among them today as a rich and acceptable sacrifice, just as you have prepared beforehand and revealed beforehand, and fulfilled, O undeceiving and true God. For this reason and for all these things I praise You, I bless You, I glorify You, through the eternal and heavenly high priest, Jesus Christ, Your beloved Son, thorough whom to You with Him and the Holy Spirit be glory now and forever. Amen."*

- When he lifted up the Amen and finished the prayer, the fire was lit. When the flame shot up, a miracle was witnessed: The fire took the form of an arch like the sail of a ship filled by the wind and encircled the body of the martyr like a wall. He was in the center of it not like burning flesh but like baking bread or like gold and silver being refined in a furnace. Those who witnessed this miracle also smelled a fragrant odor like the scent of incense or some other precious spice. When the pagans saw that his body could not be consumed by fire, they ordered the executioner to plunge a dagger into him. When he did this, a large quantity of blood came out—so much that it quenched the fire. Everyone was amazed that there was such a great difference between the unbelievers and the elect, of which Polycarp was a member. After he departed, the Jews and others created an issue over what was to be done with Polycarp's body—they thought that the faithful believers would begin to worship him, so the centurion decided to burn his body. His bones were taken up, and since that time, his martyrdom has been celebrated with joy and gladness.

Found at www.suscopts.org/stgeorgetampa/Life_of_St_Polycarp. html on 6/9/2011

WE FACE A
MEDICAL CHALLENGE

(The State Journal-Register, July 1, 2011)

The State Journal-Register's recent headline blares that "health care is poised to become top city employer." Needless to say, the forecast is a welcome news in the midst of our sluggish and anemic economic growth.

Springfield's Medical District has come a long way, indeed. It's thriving. Kudos to our community's dedicated medical professionals and their support personnel. No one doubts that we have a great health-care system, but the rest of the world is rapidly catching up with quality and affordable care.

Medical tourism is relatively a new term for traveling abroad to seek timely and affordable health care. As a case in point, thousands of Canadians leave their country each year to get their medical care elsewhere.

Unfortunately, we also face a potential challenge from practically all around the world, particularly from South Korea and Turkey to Thailand. The level of competence rivals U.S. hospitals with American-trained specialists and modern, pristine medical facilities. Plastic surgery, orthopedics (total knee and hip replacements), oral surgery (implants), and in-vitro fertilization are most vulnerable to medical tourism.

Just as our auto industry has suffered a crushing blow from its strong competitors overseas, so will our medical industry in the not distant future, unless we contain ever-rising medical costs and improve upon availability of treatment options. We just hope and pray that we will never lose out to medical tourism.

WE FACE A MEDICAL CHALLENGE

Dr. Kim, this could not have been put any better. After a serious spine injury I needed surgery to continue to walk. My surgeon was all ready to use a device that has been used for years in Europe with great results. The FDA has been reviewing the device for 20 years and has not approved it. As anyone would do, rather than sit in a chair, I went to Sweden and now I am 100%. The doctors here had only read and seen Power Points in CME on what I had done 5 years ago. America is slipping in every area, this can all be blamed on the democrats liberal government regulation and money grabbing insurance companies, not the health care providers.—Tuco23

Dr. Kim, I totally agree that the cost of health care has to be addressed. In my opinion, Democare doesn't even wave at that. Proof . . . it resembles what Canada now has and throw in MA just for good measure, along with other countries that cannot handle the growing cost. Their great idea backfired in spades.

I truly feel everyone should have access to affordable preventive health care. No offense but oral 'implants' and 'in-vitro fertilization', although important to some, do not fit under what I personally would call . . . good, basic, preventative health care, but that is me. If people want coverage, they are going to have to personally pay the premiums that coincide with that.

Until the government steps aside and lets the free market open and insurance companies actually have to compete for our needs . . . nothing will change. Let's just say I think that when Democare comes full circle, you along with the rest of us, better fasten our seat belts because we are in for a bumpy ride. Time will tell, hope I am wrong.

One last thought Dr. Kim, after reading your letter again: you state . . ."The level of competence rivals U.S. hospitals with American-trained specialists and modern pristine medical facilities" . . . then you state your entire last paragraph. I'm missing something. Are you saying that someone wanting in-vitro fertilization, for example would possibly have to fly clear across the world (to Turkey of all places) to get the best procedure or because it is as good but much cheaper than here, including all additional travel expenses? Okedoke, I'll button it up for now. Good luck to you Dr. Kim.—Mike Davis

What a waste of energy. Don't you people realize that we now have ObamaCare . . . people are never going to get sick again and everyone will become rich! Go Obama! . . . . NOT!—Anonymous

MAY JOE CLAY REST IN PEACE

(The State Journal-Register, July 20, 2011)

Dave Bakke's captivating story of Joe Clay is really heartwarming and God-sent news in this day and age.

We have gone through a very high-profile murder trial for two months, as if in a nightmare. The jury's verdict has practically split the public and a 2-year-old toddler's gruesome death still remains unresolved.

In juxtaposition to that most depressing and outrageous outcome, Joe Clay's life story sparkles a bright and shining light in the darkness. I myself know how difficult, mentally and physically draining, it is to take care of a bed-ridden patient, even for a few weeks, let alone a patient in vegetative state for 25 years.

Joe's parents, Ed and Judy, tell us their most poignant memory about what a truly caring and sacrificial love could do in a hopeless situation. Yes, Joe was cheated out of life but let us take comfort in knowing that Joe has been fed by love, breathing through love all these years.

We deeply mourn Joe's passing, extending our condolences to his parents and family. Ed and Judy are truly a role model for parents across the nation.

As for Joe, he is in heaven with the Lord, where "there will be no more death, no more grief or crying or pain." May Joe Clay rest in peace.

Reader's Response

MAY JOE CLAY REST IN PEACE

(July 21, 2011)

Dear Dr. Kim,

I found your most recent letter to be not only very well written and timely, but one that explores more deeply your own depths of emotion and caring. Also, you have given "The Kingdom" some press. I like reading this story very much.

The following key words drove the story: captivating, heart-warming, God sent, murder, toddler, gruesome, unresolved, juxtaposition, sparkles bright and shining light in the darkness, caring and sacrificial love, fed by love, breathing through love, heaven, Lord, no more death, no more grief or crying or pain.

Thank you so much for sharing,
Margaret Casey, Springfield, IL

GOOD WILL DIDN'T LAST LONG

(The State Journal-Register, August 11, 2011)

Rep. Gabrielle Giffords brought the house down when she recently returned to Congress to cast her vote for the debt limit bill.

How ironic it is that political discourse on Capitol Hill has already degenerated into a volley of invectives—some Democrats calling Republicans "terrorists waging jihad on U.S. economy" while a certain Democratic member soundly denounces the White House budget as a "sugar-coated Satan sandwich" or "a bizarre parallel universe."

Still, some other liberal opinion pieces went so far as to demand that "Tea Party members put aside their suicide vests." In the same vein, Kathleen Parker singled out, in her recent column, Tea Party members for her vengeful attack. Parker renames the Tea Party as "the Tea fraggar Party."

Across the pond, the U.K. business secretary weighed in on our debt debate that "the biggest threat to the world financial system comes from a few right-wing nutters in the American Congress rather than the euro-zone." To top it off, Russian Prime Minister Vladimir Putin has the chutzpah to dub the U.S. as "a parasite living off global economy." Pitifully, he forgets that the evil empire of the Soviet Union collapsed on its own.

Haven't we seen a gross political TV ad of a man pushing an old fragile woman in W/C off a cliff? Are we losing our minds? Do we have to make a fool of ourselves on the world stage? What happened to the civil public discourse we all clamored for, from the president on down? As they say, sticks and stones may break a bone but words can break a heart.

GOOD WILL DIDN'T LAST LONG

(August 11, 2011)

Great letter in all respects: We are told by the media constantly that we should be civil, non partisan and non ideological. Of course while we are told this Obama, the Democrats and the media trash anyone that doesn't agree with their partisan policies. Today the scapegoats are the Tea Party and S & P. Both of them are being blamed for the downgrade and the stock market collapse but let's look at the facts.

The Tea Party Republicans who were elected last November have not been responsible for any of the massive increases in spending from 2007-2011. They have not borrowed over $4 trillion dollars the last three years.

The Tea Party members were responsible for submitting the best plan for controlling the budget in the long run with Cut, Cap and Balance that would have cut a minuscule 3% of the budget in 2012. This plan was trashed by the Democrats and the media for its Draconian cuts. The Democrats are obviously the party of "no." The balance would have been stretched ten years.

Pelosi and Reid took Medicare, Medicaid and Social Security off the table and Obama took ObamaCare and Dodd Frank off the table. So which party was the party of no and was not open to compromise for much bigger budget problems.

S&P and the Tea Party are blamed for the stock market crash. It can't be the policies of Obama. It can't be the 9% unemployment, it can't be the housing crash, it can't be the massive debt in governments around the World including the U.S. Nope, it has to be the Tea Party who wants less government, less regulation and for the government to live within its means. It of course never can be Obama or the government.

John Kerry says the media should stop listening to or reporting on the Tea Party. Dissent just isn't allowed. I am glad this non partisan, civil man is on the committee to find cuts. I am sure that he is balanced in his approach. Thank goodness this man who consistently said "Assad was a reformer" is there to impart his brilliance.

Simba4hof (email response)

Unabated spending coupled with printing more money, thereby devaluing the dollar is what caused the rating drop. I read the report, and the S&P did throw some blame at Republicans for not raising taxes. As I recall, tax increases were ON the table, but when balanced by offsetting spending cuts. Reid, Pelosi and Obama took the meaningful programs off the chopping block, causing the statement and the lame agreement that came of it. Pretty simple, but the libs won't admit it, or face the consequences.

Nuff Said (email response)

OBSESSED WITH PALIN'S PLAN

(The State Journal-Register, September 2, 2011)

Kathleen Parker is at it again, railing at Sarah Palin in particular and The Tea Party in general. These days, Parker appears to be so unduly obsessed with Palin and her possible political gambits that she's got to be deep in the "trending" business. So much so she can't see things straight.

Obviously, she is now tilting at windmills. The Tea Party, despite nasty name-calling and finger-pointing from all quarters, is a purely grassroots movement backed by people in all walks of life, including Republicans and Democrats as well as Independents and transcending race and sex. Could you ever imagine the Tea Party being blamed for all our conceivable financial woes and even for Standard and Poor's downgrade of the U.S. credit rating?

Parker's strident articles in recent days remind me of a column by former Orlando Sentinel columnist Charley Reese. Their respective articles do stand in stark contrast, like day from night. Mr. Reese hung up his hat as a journalist after his 49 years of service for the Orlando Sentinel. With his master piece of work, he hits the nail on the head: according to Reese, "100 Senators, 435 in the House, 1 President and 9 Supreme Court Justices equates to 545 human beings out of 300 million—they are directly, legally, morally and individually responsible for the domestic problems that plague this country." What a revelation to us!

This Gospel truth is only a click away. Reese further argues in no uncertain terms that "politicians are the only people in the world who create problems and then campaign against them." All concerned fellow Americans, Kathleen Parker included, are well advised to read and ponder Charley Reese's column, "Why we have taxes and deficits." This is a must-read for all of us.

Editor's Note: This letter quotes a column frequently and inaccurately labeled as Charley Reese's last column. The Orlando columnist retired in 2001 and wrote his oft-cited column on deficits in 1984. Altered versions of the column circulated on the Internet during the debt ceiling debate this summer.

Reader's Response

OBSESSED WITH PALIN'S PLAN

(September 2, 2011)

Thank you for the Editor's note. Yes, there are a few versions of Mr. Reese's column . . . and they are excellent. The point is always the same . . . 'Those 545 human beings spend much of their energy convincing you that what they did is not their fault, . . . Anyone interested . . . take a look http://www.snopes.com/politics/soapbox/reese.asp. An excellent read. Slams both parties right between their eyes.

Thanks for the letter Mr. Kim. Parker, and those like her turn to the 'pen' in a desperate attempt to steer the subject matter from what is really relevant, in my opinion. The past is important to look at for guidance on what NOT to do, and the present is crucial.

We now have debt almost $17 trillion dollars and spending continues. In less than 3 years almost $7 trillion dollars was added to that debt, giving NO improvement to the economy. We have a bogus SS trust account full of IOU's and people are still told the money is there . . . and some actually believe that. Medicare and Medicaid are teetering and yet large numbers will be added to the Medicaid role . . . via ObamaCare. There are so many recent failed plans. Reese was right.

Obama will be speaking again on a Jobs Plan. I'm thrilled. He must be too as he is in NO hurry to talk about it. Before anyone jumps in and blames Boehner for asking Obama to change the date; Obama should have already had the speech considering some people actually hang on his every word.

As for what to expect . . . well I have read about his NATIONAL Infrastructure bank idea and if that doesn't send up a red flag to everyone I don't know what it is going to take. These boys and girls can't hold onto a buck let alone have any part whatsoever in anything as large as a NB. More and more government oversteps its authority and people refuse to get that it is out of control government which has caused many of our problems.

~Like it or not

I just don't understand the Lefts' "arousal" about Sarah Palin. I like a lot of her values, but just not quite sure I could vote for her as president. Only if it were Obama and her would I. The Repubs have several very good candidates vying to lead the party.

The recent comments from members of the Black Caucus against the Tea Party are so blatantly racist, yet the Liberal media doesn't call them out on this? Trying to blame the Tea Party for Black American woe is absurd. The Tea Party hasn't been around for more than three years. How can all this be their fault? Stating we want to see them hanging from a tree is pure pandering to their own race.

Let's see, who is more racist in this group: The Congressional Black Caucus or The Tea Party?

~Reality Check

OBSESSED WITH PALIN'S PLAN

(September 2, 2011)

Reality: The Republicans have tried to get an energy bill through and other jobs creating bills and Reid and Obama block them. Repealing Obamacare would help. The massive debt and deficits are destroying the economy. Thank goodness the Republicans are at least causing debate. Obama wanted an open checkbook. The Senate hasn't submitted a budget for 2.5 years and you are saying it is the Republicans who are doing nothing.

Which of Obama's policies are pro jobs, pro private sector and pro growth? Obama Care, Dodd Franks, the NLRB and EPA are destroying jobs as fast as they can. The state department has been holding up a pipeline for 2.5 years.

Obama repeatedly criticizes the Republicans for not passing the three trade agreements yet it is the Dems that have blocked the agreements since 2006 and Obama hasn't even submitted the agreements yet.

~jh1

If anyone pays attention to Ms. Parker it is their fault if they are misled. She was a total embarrassment when she was on CNN. She lives in Washington, D.C. a world all of her own. You really never know where she is coming from and which side she is on. Most people in Washington D.C. have no clue as to who and what the Tea Party really is. In my view, the Tea Partiers are just folks who are tired of high taxes, money being wasted by the Federal Government and too much government in their lives.

~lemingg

YOUNG KIM JUST LIKE FATHER

(The State Journal-Register, January 22, 2012)

Some of the events following the recent death of North Korean dictator Kim Jong II seem to be just more than a little strange. Even to a casual observer, they may be so confusing as to call for critical comments on them.

For a starter, Kim Jong Un openly flouts his grandfather's founding ideology of "Juchae" (self-reliance). As a case in point, three huge Lincoln limousines showed up at his father's funeral. Lincoln Continentals are supposed to be capitalism's status symbol as the top model of their archenemy's automakers. What's more perplexing, it is reported that luxury goods such as cars, laptops, cell phones and cigars continue to flow into North Korea despite U.N. sanctions. This enriches the lives of a growing number of their elite all the while millions of North Koreans suffer from abject poverty and massive starvation.

Back in 1983, Kim Jong II ordered a commando attack on South Korean President Chun Doo Hwan, who was visiting Rangoon. Chun was unharmed, but two of his Cabinet ministers (one of them happened to be a high school classmate of mine) and 15 other top officials perished. As if it wasn't enough, he ordered the bombing of a South Korean commercial plan that killed 115 civilians.

Like father, like son—the youngest Kim also was behind the unprovoked sinking of a South Korean warship and merciless shelling of Yeonpyeong Island last year.

In view of those relentless attacks over the years against the South, it is utterly unconscionable that the South Korean civilian delegation for Kim's funeral was headed by the former First Lady, widow of President Kim Dae-Jung. His notorious Sunshine Policy played a key role in making Pyeonyang a nuclear power in 2006.

As soon as the funeral was over, the Supreme Commander lashed out at his neighbor, threatening again to turn Seoul into "a ball of fire." But now he changes his tune, asking for U.S. food aid in exchange for suspending a uranium enrichment program. Our response should be, "Been there, done that."

Last but not least, the U.N. also made a mockery of its own charter by lowering its flags at half-staff in honor of Kim's death. The world body should be a watchdog for basic human rights, not a lapdog for dictators.

YOUNG KIM JUST LIKE FATHER

The U.N. lowers its flags whenever the ruler of a nation dies, as a common courtesy.

If the latest member of the Kim dynasty turns his palace in Pyongyang into a nuclear fireball due to inept handling of the firing button on a nuclear device, then the U.N. will lower its flags again.

Obscureknight

By the way, most of the luxury goods flow into North Korea through China, which is about the only country that still has any influence in North Korea.

North Korea will mend its ways when China tells it to mend its ways, and China will not tell North Korea to mend its ways until Japan literally performs ritual suicide and publicly apologizes for the misery that it has spread throughout Korea, Manchuria, China, the Philippines and Southeast Asia during the 1930's and the 1940's. Until Japan atones for its crimes, North Korea will remain, as a Weapon of Mass Destruction aimed at Japan, and at Japan's enabler, the USA.

Anonymous

You are our authority and information on the new leader of N. Korea. I have been wondering and hoping for a change for the people of N. Korea as they are suffering greatly due to their incarceration by the military and police. Their plight is as dire as anywhere on the planet and so I fear while the world stands by and lets this youngster have nuclear capabilities. To be so fat at 26 says a lot about the young man in this modern day. It looks as though he is petulant and self-indulgent as was his father. I think his father was diagnosable. I am praying for the boy and I call upon the people of S. Korea to pray for his conversion. If the people of N. Korea would but pray and seek the face of God, He would save them. South Korea is such a blessing. Anyway, I enjoyed your article so much and thank you for writing it. I anxiously await more articles on this subject.

Marge Casey

WISHING KIRK
SPEEDY RECOVERY

(The State Journal-Register, February 6, 2012)

The stunning news that U.S. Senator Mark Kirk suffered a stroke at age 52 out of the clear blue draws attention to internal carotid artery dissection as a cause of stroke.

Once considered uncommon, spontaneous carotid artery dissection is an increasingly recognized cause of stroke that preferentially affects the middle-aged and young people, its incidence varying anywhere from 5 percent to 20 percent. The cause can be spontaneous or traumatic.

It is also reported that minor or trivial trauma such as vomiting, coughing, and bodybuilding exercises can be implicated as a triggering mechanism of carotid artery dissection in young and healthy people. Therefore, sporting activities may place participants at some risk.

This particular type of stroke can be readily diagnosed by magnetic resonance angiography, which is considered a gold standard for its detection. As a rehab specialist, I have noted two distinct clinical features of stroke—speech impairment for right hemiplegics, which slowly improves over time with therapy, and visuo-perceptual deficits or neglect problems that somehow persist disappointingly for left hemiplegic patients.

Yet, the senator's young age and prompt surgical intervention bode well for his full recovery. We all wish him a speedy recovery with our cutting-edge rehab techniques.

TALK ABOUT A BAD SPORT

(The State Journal-Register, March 22, 2012)

The scandalous news from Massachusetts hits us like a ton of bricks; a middle school basketball coach in Springfield was officially charged with mayhem, assault, battery and disorderly conduct last week when he brutally bit off the opponent coach's ear in his fiery rage over the loss.

This is, for certain, the most bizarre and wacky incident, the like of which we have never heard of before.

Years ago, while living in Hawaii, I came across an easy-going, stout Hawaiian male whose ear was half chopped off. Curiosity got the better of me. Being directly questioned how he got hurt, he told me matter-of-factly, "One day I got drunk like a skunk and my drinking buddy bit off my poor ear while I was stoned."

I thought that the Hawaiian chap was just pulling my leg. Now, four decades later, the most unbelievable story begins to sink in with me.

If you recall, a finger-biting attack also occurred not long ago at a Tea Party rally on the West Coast.

We can't help but wonder what the world is coming to. It just seems that man bites more often than the dog, so beware of the vicious man. After all, a man-bites-dog story isn't far-fetched.

TALK ABOUT A BAD SPORT

That coach should not only be fired and imprisoned, but should be forced to payback any salary earned as a coach this year and half of all salary earned ever while coaching. There's got to be a law on (the) books for masquerading as an adult somewhere, isn't there?

FreeIllinois

SPRINGFIELDS THE WORLD OVER

(The State Journal-Register, April 22, 2012)

The State Journal-Register's April 12 "Our Opinion" prodded me to do a little Goggle search just to find out how many towns are named Springfield. Believe me, the actual number is far greater than one can imagine, with the total of 38.

I was also surprised to see that the name of Springfield is scattered practically all over the world. The United Kingdom leads the list with 15 of them, followed by Australia with seven, Canada with six and Ireland with two, New Zealand and South Africa have one each.

Which reminds me of an amusing encounter I had at an international medical symposium held by the Mayo Clinic in 1978. Looking at my name tag, a fellow attendee approached me with a smile and asked me point blank, "Are you from Springfield?" I replied, "Yes, indeed."

Then he told me he had a joke for me.

He goes, "One lady went to the train station to buy a ticket to Springfield. But the man in the booth demanded to know, "Which Springfield are you bound for, ma'am?" She shot back, "Which is the cheapest one?"

Inside joke or practical joke aside, Springfield, Ore., may have "The Simpsons." as claimed by Matt Groening, but our hometown stands head and shoulders above all the other Springfields because ours is not only the culinary home of the legendary horseshoe sandwich but also the world-renowned home of Abe Lincoln, who belong to the ages.

The Simpsons, clockwise from top left: Homer, Marge, Maggie, Santa's Little Helper, Bart, Snowball II and Lisa.

READER'S RESPONSE:

SPRINGFIELDS THE WORLD OVER

FreeIllinois

Linking the horseshoe sandwich and Abe Lincoln is about as close to a visual oxymoron that I can imagine.

Adding french fries from the closest greasy frying vat to a sandwich and then slopping it with cheese as the height of culinary achievement? At first I thought Dr. Kim was being sarcastically funny, or he's running for office. hahaha. I guess it's possible to be genuine in those sentiments.

I wonder if knowing that Springfield didn't vote for Lincoln during his presidential elections or that Springfield once named John Wayne Gacy as the town's Man of the Year would influence his opinion?

Good conversation over a 'ponyshoe' perhaps?

BobJudd/Chatam
A good letter but you left out a few informational tips for the future tourists wanting to visit this particular Springfield in Illinois. Besides being "the culinary home of the legendary horseshoe sandwich" (a great dish) and being "the world-renowned home of Abe Lincoln," who belongs to the ages.

It's also the home of the Convention Center that was voted down by the Citizens whose wishes were completely ignored -- As they usually are.

It's also home to the Abe Lincoln Hotel that was the result of a corrupt transaction (made possible by political contributors) that also belongs to the ages.

It's also the home of the state capitol where the Illinois State Legislatures are famously bought and sold with P.A.C. (BRIBE) money.

It's also the training headquarters for past and future Politicians -- especially Governors -- wanting to reside in our famous prison system.

It is also the home of the deadbeat State Legislature that is so far in debt it can't pay its bills or pay into the retirement pensions of its employees.

ABOUT THE AUTHOR

Dr. Chansoo Kim was born on September 13, 1937 in Taegu, Korea. He received his M.D. Degree in 1963 from Kyungpook University School of Medicine in his home town. Residency in Physical Medicine and Rehabilitation at New York University Medical Center—Bellevue Hospital, New York City, N.Y. Teaching Fellow, Institute of Rehab Medicine, New York University Medical Center. Associate Professor of Physical Medicine and Rehab (PM&R), University of Hawaii Postgraduate Medical Education Program, Ryukyu Islands (before Reversion to Japan). Associate Medical Director, Pacific Institute of Rehab. Medicine (PIRM), Honolulu, Hawaii (Currently, Rehabilitation Hospital on Pacific). Chairman of Department of Rehab Medicine, Memorial Medical Center, Springfield, IL followed by private practice in Springfield, IL. Presently, Physician Consultant for the State of Illinois. Dr. Kim is licensed in the states of Hawaii, Illinois, New York, as well as Korea and Okinawa (Japan). He holds membership with the American Medical Association (AMA), the American Academy of Physical Medicine and Rehab (Fellow), the American Congress of Rehab. Medicine, the Illinois State Medical Society, the Sangamon County Medical Society and the American Association of Neuromuscular and Electrodiagnostic Medicine (Emeritus Member) and the American Dialect Society.